GROCERY
MATH!

The Whimsical Logic of Retail, Relationships, and Reality Checks

After you decode the humor in every Girl Math rule, sharing your thoughts would be super cool!

Leave a Rating or a Review!

Scan Here

Table of Contents

Get ready to laugh, learn, and justify!

Introduction

Unveiling the Quirky World of Girl Math

Girl Math isn't about numbers or equations—it's about the creative and sometimes absurd ways we navigate through life's decisions and dilemmas. It's the mental gymnastics we perform to rationalize choices. And while this book may not capture every Girl Math rule out there, know that there are unlimited examples waiting to be discovered in the wilds of everyday life.

While the term may suggest it's exclusive to girls, it's far from it. Girl Math is a universal phenomenon, but it's often girls who revel in its playful logic and imaginative reasoning.

At its core, Girl Math celebrates the fun and charm in our thought processes—the unique ways we justify actions, make sense of the world, and find humor in the absurdity of it all. It's not about gender stereotypes but rather about embracing the delightful idiosyncrasies of human nature.

As we explore the whimsical world of Girl Math, remember that it's about laughing at our own contradictions and finding joy in the unexpected twists and turns of life. After all, when we reflect on our lives, we won't regret the Girl Math we used; we'll regret the Girl Math we failed to embrace. So, let's dive in and unravel the delightful mysteries of Girl Math together!

girl math (n.) /ɡərl mæθ/

the mental gymnastics performed by individuals to rationalize decisions, often involving creative calculations, emotional factors, and a dash of whimsy

Chapter 1:
Retail Therapy and Fashion Fables

Rule # 1

Cash Is Not Real Money

"I treat cash like Monopoly money— it's a game and I'm winning!"

—— The Logic ——

If it doesn't dent the account, it doesn't count!

When you're dealing with cash, it's like playing a sneaky game of hide and seek with your bank account. You hand over those paper bills, and bam – no record, no trace, like it never even happened. Cash is like the invisible ink of money; spend it, and who's to know?

Here's the quirky math: If cash leaves your wallet but doesn't show up in your bank statement, did you really spend it? It's obviously not going to stay in your wallet forever, so does it matter when it leaves? Handing over cash is like whispering a secret to the cashier – "Here, take this, and let's never speak of it again." Your bank account stays just as plump and happy, blissfully unaware of your little cash adventures. It's like what happens in Vegas stays in Vegas, but with your wallet.

But remember, when the cash is gone, it's gone. Poof! Vanished! Like a magician's rabbit or your motivation on a Monday. But who cares? It was fun while it lasted, right? Just like that carnival ride you know you shouldn't go on, but you do anyway because YOLO. So next time you break a fifty, don't stress. It's just cash – the money that comes and goes as mysteriously as your socks in the laundry.

Rule# 2

Credit Cards Are Not Real Money

"Credit cards are like those free trial subscriptions, right? Fun now, worry later!"

—— The Logic ——

Tapping's too easy to make costs feel queasy!

Alright, so we just decided cash is basically monopoly money, right? Well, credit cards are even more out there! It's a piece of plastic pretending to be money. You swipe, and poof – stuff becomes yours, but your wallet feels just as heavy. If cash is play money, credit cards are imaginary. Tap! Are you kidding me?

Of course, swiping that credit card is like living in a dreamy bubble of "That's Future Me's problem." The beauty? Your bank account isn't immediately hit; it's like a magical delay. When you use a credit card, those dollars float away like bubbles, not really feeling real because, hey, your bank balance doesn't budge.

The thought that you could just say, "Eh, I'll deal with it later" is weirdly comforting. It's the financial version of snoozing your alarm – sure, you'll have to wake up eventually, but for now, just keep dreaming!

Each credit card transaction is a tiny vacation from reality. You're not just buying things; you're buying time from facing the music. Just remember, every 'snooze' comes to an end, and that credit card bill is the ultimate wake-up call. But until then, enjoy the fantasy where your bank account and your shopping spree live in blissful, separate worlds!

Rule# 3
Gift Cards Definitely
Aren't Real Money

"Gift cards are just fancy coupons that mean shop till you drop!"

—— The Logic ——

Plastic for something real? Feels like a steal!

Gift cards are like getting a VIP ticket to Spendville – they're not your cash, they're not your credit, they're just this fun shopping pass! It's like someone handed you a "Go Crazy" card. You can't make them feel like real money even if you tried.

Using a gift card feels like a mini triumph. Why? Because let's face it, we often forget to use them. So, when you actually remember to spend one, it's like giving yourself a pat on the back. You're not just spending; you're rescuing this little card from being forgotten in the depths of your wallet. It's a feel-good moment, turning what could have been a wasted gift into a shopping victory!

The joy of spending a gift card is twofold. First, there's no tally running in your head, no mental math subtracting from your bank account. It's your guilt-free pass to splurge city. Second, by using it, you're making the gift even more meaningful. It's like honoring the giver's intention – "Look, I'm actually enjoying what you gave me!"

But, as with all good things, there's a limit. The shopping euphoria lasts until you hit that tragic number- zero, it's a gentle nudge back to the land of budgeting and responsible spending. But until then, revel in the joy of playing in the realm of "This was a gift, and I'm making the most of it!"

Rule# 4

The Investment Illusion

"This designer bag isn't just a purse; it's my retirement plan!"

—— The Logic ——

When the cost is grand, we're in investment land!

Labeling a splurge as an 'investment' is the ultimate financial flip. High-end gadget? That's not a splurge; it's an investment in tech-savviness. Designer jewelry? New family heirloom! And that luxury car? It's an investment in road safety and, um, prestige.

The beauty of the 'investment' label is its magical ability to turn even the guiltiest pleasure into a wise, long-term decision. The more zeros on the price tag, the bigger the 'investment' sounds. You aren't just "spending," you're strategically allocating resources for future happiness!

Let's be real, anything that makes you gulp at the price is ripe for the investment label. It's like giving your conscience a soothing pat on the back – "Don't worry, it's for the future." Whether it's a gadget that'll be outdated by next year or shoes you'll wear once, in the moment, it feels like you're planning for a better tomorrow.

But remember, the 'investment' justification has its limits. It works wonders at easing the immediate spend-guilt, but when the credit card bill arrives, it might just ask, "So, how's that investment working out for you?" Until that reality check, though, bask in the glory of your oh-so-wise 'investments' that make today just a little more fabulous!

Rule# 5
Earning Store Credit Is Profiting

"Returning my fashion fumble for store credit is like recycling while profiting!"

——— The Logic ———

Store credit's a mandate to spree, forget where it came from, it's free!

When you return something for store credit, boom, you just bagged a profit! Nevermind whatever you originally paid. That's in the past, and store credit is the ultimate mindtrap in the world of shopping. It's a refund that's not quite money, but still spends like it. It's not just your right to buy something else, it's now your obligation.

The mental loop-de-loop is clear: since it's not coming directly from your bank account, it feels less like spending and more like using a coupon. With every extravagant item you consider, your mind vaults over the usual budget bars. "Would I buy this with my own money?" becomes a distant thought, replaced by, "Well, it's store credit, so why not?" It's a liberating leap from your usual spending habits, a cartwheel out of the mundane and into the extraordinary.

But beware, the final act of this shopping circus comes at the checkout. That's when you stick the landing and realize your store credit started a shopping chain reaction. Your wallet joins the performance, and suddenly, you're spending more than the store credit's worth.

Let's just conveniently forget about the original spending that earned the store credit. Don't we love our backflips of rationalization?

Rule# 6

Price Tag Amnesia

"I got an overpriced throw pillow, but with the price tag gone, it's just cozy elegance."

—— The Logic ——

Price tag remorse is easy to evade, just rip it off fast like a bandaid!

Once you rip off that price tag, it's like the cost never existed. Think of it as a financial cleanse – no tag, no record, no fretting over the numbers. If the amount you spent bothers you, girl, just swiftly tear it off, and poof, the spending guilt vanishes into thin air.

It's like removing a tiny little anchor to reality. The moment that tag hits the trash, the memory of what you spent fades away--a magic trick for your wallet's conscience. You had to remove the tag anyway, right? Might as well use it as a mini therapy session for your buyer's remorse.

The beauty of this approach lies in its simplicity. You're not just physically separating the item from its cost; you're mentally detaching from the price. The price tag is gone, and with it, any lingering thoughts of, "Should I have really bought this?"

Until your monthly bill arrives, bask in the ignorant bliss of your tag-free treasure. After all, what's a little fiscal amnesia if it brings you joy?

Rule# 7

The Cart-Fill Fantasy

"Wow, those boots look amazing, better add to cart now just in case!"

—— The Logic ——

Nothing wrong with adding to cart, because at checkout, I'll be smart!

While online shopping, filling up your cart is basically a no-risk game. It's like window shopping, but digital. Each addition to the cart is like a little "what if" without any real commitment. It's the thrill of the hunt, with none of the wallet's bite.

This Cart-Fill Fantasy is simple: Add to Cart = Zero Harm. It's like building a dream castle in the cloud, where every item is a brick of wishful thinking. You're not spending money; you're curating possibilities. It's a harmless hover in the land of maybe, where everything is just a click away from being real.

Hovering over that 'Proceed to Checkout' button, though, that's where the fantasy ends and reality begins. But until you make that final click, it's all just a fun game of make-believe shopping. So go ahead, fill that cart to the brim, play with the endless combinations of 'could-bes' and 'might-looks-greats'. It's the safest spree you'll ever have – until, of course, it isn't. Just remember, the cart is your playground, and the checkout is the principal's office!

Rule# 8

The Rewards Points Paradox

"Every purchase on my platinum card is a step closer to my dream vacation, one shoe at a time!"

—— The Logic ——

If you earn points by spending a lot, you can pretend it's a saving plot.

With Girl Math principles at play, any purchase, no matter how grand, is totally justifiable as long as it racks up those sweet, sweet rewards points. It's the Rewards Points Paradox – where the splurge becomes a savvy move, as long as there's a promise of points.

It works like this: You see something extravagant, your wallet winces, but then – aha! The rewards points come into play. Suddenly, that pricey item isn't just a purchase; it's a strategic move in the game of points accumulation. It's not about the money spent; it's about the points earned. The more you spend, the more you earn, and therefore, the more you save (kind of, sort of, not really, but let's go with it).

This principle turns every shopping spree into a quest for rewards glory. It's like a points-collecting marathon, where each swipe of your card gets you closer to that coveted reward – be it airline miles, cashback, or some. The paradox lies in the mental gymnastics of justifying lavish spending as a form of saving. So, the next time you're eyeing something with a hefty price tag, remember the Rewards Points Paradox. With the right amount of mental squinting, every extravagant buy becomes a step towards victory in the points chase.

Rule # 9

The Free Shipping Fallacy

"Shipping's $8? I'll just add four more tops to get free shipping!"

—— The Logic ——
If it helps you skip the shipping fee, the next add to cart is practically free!

In the savvy shopper's handbook, paying for shipping is practically a cardinal sin. Enter the Free Shipping Fallacy: why pay for delivery when you can just add more stuff to your cart? It's a simple mental mandate for all Girl Math subscribers-- buy enough to earn free shipping no matter the cost.

This strategy is genius in its simplicity. You're at checkout, and there's a shipping charge staring you down. But wait – add a little more to the cart, and suddenly, shipping's on the house! You found a cheat code to savings. You're not spending more; you're strategically avoiding an extra cost. It's Girl Math at its finest – spend more, save more.

Just remember, the Free Shipping Fallacy can turn your quick shopping trip into a treasure hunt for items you didn't know you needed. But that's better than paying for something that you can't even try on in front of your full body mirror, right?

Rule# 10

Compliments are Currency

"A compliment on my new outfit is basically a full rebate!"

—— The Logic ——

Every "You look great!"
offsets the cost at any rate!

The Compliment Currency rule is like a golden rule in the fashion world. It states that if your new purchase earns you compliments, then whatever you paid for it is totally, absolutely worth it. It's like your outfit has its own return on investment, measured in "oohs" and "aahs" instead of dollars and cents.

This formula works like charm. You might splurge on something fancy and then have a tiny moment of "Did I really need this?" But the moment someone says, "Wow, I love what you're wearing!", it's all validated. It's as if each compliment is a little deposit back into your style bank, replenishing what you spent.

The more people admire your purchase, the more valuable it feels. And it's not just about feeling good; it's about that sweet vindication. Every "You look great!" is like a tick in the 'worth it' column.

So, next time you buy something that makes your wallet wince, just wait for the compliments to roll in. With Compliment Currency, you're investing in your personal stock of fabulousness. You're transforming money into wearable confidence, and that is priceless.

Rule# 11
Shopping Bag Workout

"The more shopping bags I carry at the mall, the more tone my arms will get!"

—— The Logic ——

Shop more, lift more,
it's the perfect score!

Next time you hit the mall, remember: every shopping bag you carry is helping you craft your ideal physique. More Bags = Better Workout. Think of each bag as a weight, and the mall as your track – you're basically a shopping athlete in training!

Consider picking up those bags early in your shopping trip and make them count; the longer you carry them, the more calories you burn. Heavier bags equal a more intense workout – it's like weightlifting with a retail twist. As you weave through the stores, every step is a calorie burned, every bag a muscle toned. It's a practical application of physics – weight resistance meets endurance.

So, embrace the burn as you trot from store to store. Each additional purchase isn't just an item; it's an added pound to your impromptu workout regime. And by the time you've navigated the entire mall, you've not only aced your shopping goals but also hit a day's worth of exercise.

Rule # 12

The Double Duty Discount

"Thought the velvet blazer was too pricey, but it's reversible? That's like BOGO!"

—— The Logic ——

If it's two in one, it's like half the price... and double the fun!

Girl Math can help you justify any purchase where the product serves double duty. Reversible jackets and all-in-one dresses are obvious clever savings strategies. When you snag a reversible jacket, it's like getting two trendy looks for the price of one. Flip it inside out, and voila – new jacket, who dis? The same goes for dresses – they're a top and bottom combined, which, in Girl Math, means a 50% discount.

So if the price tag makes you sweat, just remember, if it's a multitasker, do some quick Girl Math and imagine that price tag in half.

Also, think of the time and effort saved. A reversible jacket means less decision-making in the morning. As for dresses, they're the ultimate 'hit that snooze button' outfit. No matching, no mixing, just slip on and go.

In Girl Math, it's not about how much you spend; it's about how smartly you spend. And who knows, maybe this rule will extend to other clothing pieces – because in Girl Math, the only thing better than a great outfit is a great outfit that's secretly two.

Rule# 13

The Essential Extras Equation

"Buying a cute fit without matching boots is like having a phone with no internet!"

—— The Logic ——

An outfit's just the start, accessories make the art!

It's all about accessorizing. If you don't have all the accessories you crave, it's like you've only done half the job on your outfit. You've got a chic dress? Great start. But leave behind those stunning shoes or that must-have necklace, and girl, you're doing the math all wrong.

Imagine this: You score an adorable top, but then you skip the matching scarf that just screams your name. That's like baking a cake and not eating it – what's the point? Accessories are the exclamation marks of your outfit equation; they're what take your style statement from a whisper to a shout.

In the world of Girl Math, combining an outfit with accessories isn't just addition; it's a style multiplication! It's the kind of math where the whole is definitely greater than the sum of its parts. So, the next time you're out shopping, remember to complete the equation. Your closet isn't just a collection of clothes; it's a treasure trove of style opportunities, waiting to be perfectly paired. It's the extras that count.

Rule # 14
The Sale Paradox

"Picked up a $200 jacket for $50 – I basically earned $150!"

—— The Logic ——

Every sale tag = money—saving brag!

Embrace the Sale Paradox, where every markdown is a mark-up in your savings account – at least in the wonderland of shopping math. If it's on sale, you're not just spending; you're practically earning!

Imagine this: a gorgeous jacket, originally priced at a small fortune, now 75% off. You didn't just save 75%; you 'earned' it. It's a fantastic fiscal flip where the focus shifts from what you spend to what you've 'gained'.

This is a masterclass in self-deception and delight. Each sale tag is like a sly wink from the universe, promising a deal too good to be true. And let's be real, we know deep down that 'original prices' might just be a retail fairy tale, yet we happily play along. It's like believing in Santa – a little bit make-believe, a little bit magic.

So, when you next see that 'Sale' sign, dive into the Sale Paradox with eyes wide open. Sure, we might be kidding ourselves believing in those inflated original prices, but who cares? It's an opportunity to indulge in a little financial fantasy, transforming spending into saving in a blink of an eye. Every marked-down price tag is like finding money you never knew you lost!.

Rule # 15

Last Item Serendipity

"Only one more yoga mat in my fave color. It's the universe saying, 'Yes, you need more yoga.'"

—— The Logic ——

I know it's divine, when the last item's mine!

When you find the last one of anything in a store, it's not just luck; it's cosmic alignment. That last item sitting there? It's like the universe has reserved it just for you. Picture this: You're browsing, and there it is – the last one of its kind. It's like finding a four-leaf clover. Sure, the rational side of you knows it's just inventory, but the shopper in you hears destiny calling. Don't question it, it is a sign.

It's almost as if your guardian angel is playing personal shopper. Picture your angel, hovering in the aisles, gently steering other shoppers away, ensuring this last treasure waits just for you. It's a celestial reserve, a divine hold. As you reach out and take that last item, it's like a quiet high-five with your guardian angel. They've been looking out for you, setting aside this special piece in the grand cosmic inventory. It's a little wink from above, a nudge that says, "I got you."

Ignoring it is defying fate. You wouldn't want to upset the shopping gods, would you? So, when you come across that last piece, repeat this in your head, "Yes, this is meant to be." It's the universe's way of pointing you in the right direction.

Oops, there's two left? One for the bestie!

Rule# 16

Hesitation Inflation

"I waited on the concert tickets and the price tripled! Better get them now before it happens again!"

—— The Logic ——

Every hold off today is just tomorrow's dismay!

You find that perfect sparkly dress. It's shining under the store lights, practically calling your name. But then, oh no, you decide to 'think about it'. Fast forward to a week later, and that dress is now a mythical creature you can't find or afford. It's like it grew wings and flew right off to someone else's closet. Now you're not just dress-less; you're full of regret and probably buying a consolation scarf you don't need.

Hesitation Inflation is like the boogeyman of the shopping world – wait too long and poof, the price tag grows or, worse, your dream item vanishes! It's a universal law in the retail universe: the longer you wait, the more expensive (emotionally and wallet-ly) it gets.

Is this 'price increase' more in our heads than in reality? Maybe, but it's like there's a tiny shopping fairy whispering, "Buy it now, or it'll cost you your happiness later!" And let's be honest, who can argue with a shopping fairy?

The next time you're contemplating that 'maybe' purchase, remember the Hesitation Inflation rule. It's way better to be the gal who snagged that sparkly dressing, instead of the one sobbing about 'the one that got away'.

Rule # 17

The Coupon Code Commandment

"I was pretty sure it was time to get an espresso machine, but when I found a 20% off promo, I had no doubt! "

—— The Logic ——

Finding a promo code isn't just great, it's totally fate!

The Coupon Code Commandment is like the ultimate green light at checkout. Find a code, and suddenly, not buying feels like breaking a universal law. It's a fun little twist in the online shopping plot: find a discount code, and boom, you're practically obligated to use it.

You're online shopping and eyeing that fancy blender or those trendy boots, but the price is making you hesitate. Then, as if by magic (or a quick web search), a wild promo code appears! Suddenly, the universe seems to be saying, "I mean, you HAVE to buy it now." It's like finding a secret key to the discount kingdom.

We all know deep down this is just our inner shopaholic looking for a sign, any sign, to click 'buy'. But the moment that code works, it feels like destiny. The shopping stars have aligned, and who are we to mess with cosmic fate?

Next time you stumble upon a promo code after a casual Google search, remember the Coupon Code Commandment. Your "maybe" just got turned into a "definitely." Not only did you dodge guilt, but you also earned a pat on the back for your savvy shopping skills!

Rule # 18
Retail is Cheaper than Real Therapy

"Buying new clothes makes me happy, so it's saving money because I'm not in therapy!"

—— The Logic ——
You can't take therapy home, better to find a store to roam!

Why pay for a therapist when a shopping spree offers the same uplift, but with wardrobe benefits? It's like choosing between talking out your feelings and walking out with bags full of joy. It's the ultimate two-for-one deal – you avoid the hourly rates and judgmental looks of a therapist, and in return, you get mood-boosting merchandise.

Feeling down? A new pair of shoes might just lift your spirits. Stressful day? That new handbag suddenly seems like a wise investment in your mental health. Shopping can be just as effective as traditional therapy, minus the couch. And let's face it, a shopping spree is way more fun than spilling your guts to a stranger, who, you know deep down your significant-other needs more than you.

So, next time life throws you a curveball, remember therapy is a short, spur-of-the-moment drive away. It's a wink at the notion that sometimes, the best way to deal with life's ups and downs is to indulge in a little retail rendezvous. What better band-aid for the soul than a shopping bag?

Rule# 19

The Fashion Familiarity Formula

"My new top just got Instagram tagged, so I guess that's the end of its runway."

—— The Logic ——

If you show it too often, the glam will soften!

The Fashion Familiarity Formula operates on a simple but brutal truth: the more a piece is seen, the faster its style stock plummets. Wear it once, and its fashion value drops by half. If someone else is spotted in the same outfit? Well, it might as well be relegated to closet obscurity, only to be resurrected for a paint day or a DIY disaster.

Imagine you debut a stunning new dress at a party. It's a hit, and you feel like a million bucks. But the next time you wear it, the compliments are fewer, the glances less admiring. In the world of fashion, familiarity breeds indifference. It's as if each outing of an outfit erodes its wow factor, depreciating its style currency.

Now, let's add another twist. You see someone else rocking the same dress. Suddenly, it's like all the air's been let out of your fashion balloon. It's no longer your unique statement; it's just part of the fashion masses.

The Fashion Familiarity Formula is a guiding principle for the style-savvy. It dictates a constant refresh of your wardrobe, pushing you to stay ahead in the fashion race. In the couture ecosystem, novelty reigns supreme. If you keep them guessing, you'll keep them admiring.

Rule# 20

Anything Under $5 is Free

"A $4 mug? If it's cheaper than my latte, not even a double shot can wake my worries!"

—— The Logic ——

Less than five barely makes the archive!

For anything under five dollars, it's less about the price tag and more about, "Do I really want another cute but utterly unnecessary knick-knack in my life?" Spoiler alert: The answer is usually a resounding "Yes!"

Picture this: I'm wandering through the dollar store, a wonderland where everything's a steal. I spot this adorable little succulent in a teeny tiny pot. Price? A whopping $1.50. "Do I need it? No. Do I want it? Absolutely. Will it clutter my already crowded shelf? Probably. But hey, it's less than a coffee!"

This rule is like navigating a minefield of miniature temptations, and, OMG, shopping at the dollar store is like being a kid in a candy shop. You have way too much going on to worry about the cost of anything at the dollar store!

So, next time you find yourself holding a trinket or a gadget that's under five bucks, remember, if it's that cheap, you literally don't have time to think about the price. And if your home slowly transforms into a cluttered shrine of these mini freebies, just throw it all away, it was free anyway!

Fun Fact:

Women control 85% of consumer spending.

We're not shopaholics; we're economic influencers!

Source: Forbes (2019)

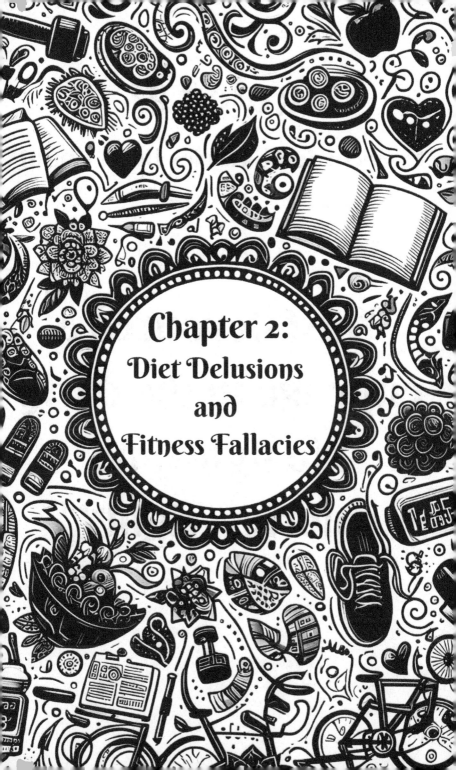

Chapter 2:
Diet Delusions
and
Fitness Fallacies

Rule# 21

Unrecorded Calories Don't Count

"Just devoured a cupcake in the dark. No lights, no calories, right?"

—— The Logic ——

If I don't jot it down, it won't add a pound!

Girl Math allows for blissful denial in calorie counting. If you didn't record on your calorie counting app, did you really eat it? It's a comforting loophole for all those sneaky snacks. When there's no record, it's like those calories just floated away into thin air, leaving no trace on your diet diary or your waistline.

Now, let's dive into the nocturnal variant: Drunk Eating. The rule here is simple yet wonderfully convenient – if you can't recall eating it, your body definitely can't either. It's like a mysterious calorie amnesia. Had a late-night pizza after a few drinks? If your memory's foggy, your body's record-keeping is supposedly just as hazy.

Of course, deep down, we all know the truth: the body isn't fooled so easily. But in the lighthearted spirit of Girl Math, who's to argue with a little selective amnesia now and then? It's like giving yourself a free pass from the strict world of calorie tracking. The next time you find yourself indulging in a midnight feast or forgetting to jot down that extra slice of cake, just remember this rule.

Rule# 22

The Pre-Diet Binge Boost

"I'm eating a ton today so I'll have the guilt I need to power through my keto diet!"

—— The Logic ——

A feast before fast, makes the healthy habits last!

The Pre-Diet Binge Boost operates on a deliciously deceptive premise: the more you indulge today, the more motivated you'll be to start that diet tomorrow. It's a classic case of culinary carpe diem, mixed with a dash of tomorrow's optimism.

You're about to start a diet, but suddenly, every treat looks extra tempting. So, you think, "Why not go all out today? It'll just make me more determined to be good starting tomorrow." It's like revving up for a race with a feast – the fuller you are today, the faster you'll run towards those salad greens tomorrow, right?

Deep down, we all know it's a bit of a stretch. Yet, there's something so appealing about this last-hurrah mentality. It's like giving yourself a farewell party from the world of indulgence, believing it'll turbocharge your willpower for the dieting journey ahead. It's the Fat Tuesday of Girl Math dieting.

So, the next time you find yourself justifying an extra slice of cake or a second helping of pasta with the feast today, fast tomorrow logic, chuckle at the fallacy and enjoy the moment. After all, in the grand buffet of life, sometimes the promise of 'starting tomorrow' is just the excuse we need for a little extra joy on our plates today!

Rule# 23

The Calorie Count Carryover

"Office donuts? Oh yeah, I missed dinner, so it's fine!"

—— The Logic ——

Yesterday's meal skip justifies today's flavor trip!

You know how some days are just non-stop, and you completely forget to eat? Yeah, me neither, but let's pretend. On those rare, probably fictional days, you end up not consuming all your allocated calories. This creates a calorie surplus – kind of like rollover data, but instead of extra gigabytes, it's just bites!

It's Wednesday, and you've somehow managed to skip lunch because you were deep in a YouTube rabbit hole of watching cats play piano – happens to the best of us. Those uneaten lunch calories are now stored in your calorie bank, earning interest overnight. Now, it's Thursday, and you're eyeing that double chocolate fudge cake. Normally, your inner health guru might say, "Hey, maybe not," but thanks to yesterday's lunch-skipping escapade, your inner guru is more like, "You've earned this, champion."

Now, I know what you're thinking: "Is this how nutrition works?" And to that, I say, "Shh, let's not ruin this with science."Girl Math is not about the accuracy; it's about the feeling.

So next time you skip a meal by accident (or on purpose – no judgment), remember this rule. It's your free pass to indulge without the bulge, a magical math that turns missed meals into guilt-free deals. Just remember to spend those rollover calories wisely – or don't, I'm not your calorie accountant!

Rule # 24

Homemade Equals Healthy Rule

"I made brownies with almond flour and agave nectar. I just love guilt-free health bars!"

— The Logic —

If it's not dining out, it's healthy, no doubt!

Anything you whip up in your kitchen is inherently healthier than what you'd get outside. Homemade cookies? So all-natural. Lasagna from scratch? You can't eat any better! This rule is like culinary rose-colored glasses. As soon as an apron is donned, calories seem to magically diminish. Butter is just a love ingredient, sugar becomes sweet well-wishes, and cheese – it's practically a health food when it's grated by your own hands.

The charm of this rule is in its creative accounting. Every dollop of cream or sprinkle of sugar gets a health pass because, hey, it's made with love, right? The "homemade" label is like a magic spell that transforms every dish into a potion of well-being.

Deep down we know better. Sure, a home-cooked meal can be healthier, but when your version of spaghetti Bolognese is 50% pasta, 50% cheese, and a whisper of tomato sauce, it's a stretch to call it a balanced meal. But hey, if you chopped the onions yourself, it counts as a workout, right?

It's a bit like believing wearing sneakers makes you instantly athletic. In the great cookbook of life, sometimes the recipe for happiness includes a pinch of delusion, especially if it's served right from your stove. After all, who's counting calories when there's love (and a little extra cheese) in every bite?

Rule# 25

Protein Equals Health Hypothesis

"If I dust my ice cream with vanilla protein powder, it's fueling my muscles!

—— The Logic ——

You can be a total fatass
if protein's there to give it a pass!

It seems impossible to not believe it, even if it's a twist in dietary logic: as long as a dish is packed with enough protein, it's magically transformed into a health food. Making brownies? Just add a scoop of protein powder. Pancakes? They're a bodybuilder's dream with a scoop of the good stuff. It's like wearing gym clothes all day and feeling fitter for it.

This hypothesis turns every meal into a healthful feast with just a protein punch. It's a culinary flex that bends the rules of nutrition – who knew that a sprinkle of protein could rewrite a dish's dietary story? A milkshake becomes a muscle shake, and suddenly, that spaghetti with protein pasta is a power meal.

It's a bit like putting racing stripes on a car and feeling the speed increase – the protein boost doesn't erase the sugar or carbs, but it sure adds a veneer of health. It's nutritional optimism at its finest: if it's protein-rich, it's guilt-free, right? We all need our fun ways to give our favorite foods a health halo, even if it's a bit of a dietary stretch.

Rule# 26
The Rep Round-Up Rule

"7 reps in, I remembered math class – always round up, so I definitely did 10."

—— The Logic ——

A little cheat makes the rep count sweet!

This one is a gem in the gym-goer's playbook: when it comes to counting reps, rounding up is not just allowed, it's encouraged. Did seven squats? In the world of Girl Math, that's basically ten. It's a feel-good numerical nudge that turns every exercise session into a triumph.

This rule is the fitness equivalent of 'close enough.' It's for those moments when you're gasping for breath, muscles burning, and you manage to eke out just a few reps. But in the grand scheme of things, isn't seven just a stone's throw away from ten? It's a rounding practice that adds a dash of pride to your sweat and toil.

Think of it as creative accounting for your fitness regimen. It's like giving yourself a pat on the back for effort. Sure, the numbers might be a bit fuzzy, but what counts is the spirit behind them. After all, in the grand narrative of fitness, isn't it the effort that truly counts?

What's wrong with a little bit of self-encouragement, a way to make each session feel like a bigger win? Sometimes rounding up is just the motivational boost you need. After all, isn't every round-up a step closer to your goals, whether it's seven, ten, or whatever?

Rule# 27

Set Count Supremacy

"You don't need a calculator to know that 5 sets of 3 squats is better than 4 sets of 6!"

—— The Logic ——

If it feels like more, then it's a score!

You've heard of 4x6 being the sweet spot, right? Well, hold onto your protein shakers, because 5x3 is the new black.

Imagine me, strutting into the gym with the confidence of someone who believes avocado toast is a full meal. Who cares if traditional wisdom says 3x10 is double the reps? In my gym diary, 5x3 is the sparkling diamond. Why do a quick 3x10 when I can take my time with a 5x3? Fewer reps makes each one feel like a mini victory, and by the time I hit the third one, I'm ready to take a bow.

"Why push through ten when you can triumph in three?" I muse as I effortlessly transition from weights to the water cooler. Each sip tastes like victory—a victory flavored with the sweet essence of minimal effort for maximal satisfaction.

Wrapping up my session, the gym mirrors reflect a conqueror, someone who took the road less rep-ed and made it her runway. In the gym, as in life, sometimes less is more, and smart beats hard.

Set Count Supremacy may not make me the strongest person in the gym, but it certainly makes me the smuggest. Just don't try to apply this math to your taxes; turns out, the IRS doesn't appreciate creative arithmetic quite as much.

Rule# 28

The Checkin Workout

"Selfie with the treadmill means I've basically run a mile, right?"

—— The Logic ——

The workout ain't wrapped until the selfie's snapped!

Where sweat is the currency and muscles are the return on investment, there lies a secret shortcut to success: the checkin workout. Yes, simply checking into the gym on your social media platform of choice is the equivalent of a full workout. And if you manage to snap a selfie, you've just doubled your workout efficiency without so much as lifting a finger (well, except to tap your screen).

Upon entering the gym, the first step is not to reach for a dumbbell or mount the treadmill. Oh no, it's to whip out your phone and check in on social media. This act alone sends shockwaves through your social network, signaling that you are, indeed, a person of iron will and unmatched discipline.

Now, for the pièce de résistance: the gym selfie. This isn't just any selfie; it's a carefully orchestrated piece of performance art. The angle, the smize, the casual yet deliberate positioning of gym equipment in the background—it all contributes to the illusion of a grueling workout session.

If we subscribe to the idea that perception is reality, then truly, my strategically angled selfie are as valid as any sweat-drenched hour on the elliptical. Just don't forget to occasionally lift something heavier than your smartphone—your followers need to believe you're actually capable of it, after all.

Rule# 29

The Diet Drink Deduction

"A coke zero with my large fries means I'm practically eating air, right? Science."

—— The Logic ——

With a diet drink in hand, your meals can expand!

The Diet Drink Deduction is a beacon of hope for those of us navigating the tumultuous seas of indulgence and restraint. It's the belief, nay, the certainty, that pairing a diet drink with less healthy food options magically neutralizes the calories. It's like wearing black—it just slims everything down.

Your heart says, "Let's get that triple-layer cheeseburger," but your brain says, "Remember the beach body?" Just as you're about to resign yourself to a salad (sigh), a lightbulb moment: order a diet soda with it, and voilà, balance is restored.

This principle is built on the bedrock of Girl Math, a complex algorithm that calculates that the lack of calories in a diet drink cancel out the positive calories of a cheese-laden mega meal. Never mind the side of fries; they're just there for emotional support. The soda sips whisper, "You're doing great, sweetie," with every greasy, glorious bite. It's a perfect blend of flavors and faux health.

So next time you find yourself facing a dietary crossroads, remember: a diet drink doesn't just quench your thirst, it paves the way for culinary indulgence. And if anyone questions your methods, just tell them you're on a balanced diet—half diet soda, half pizza, perfectly aligned in gastronomic harmony.

Rule# 30

Activewear Activation Theory

"Just by wearing leggings, it's leg day; muscles tone without a single squat!"

—— The Logic ——

When the outfit's tight, the muscles ignite!

With Girl Math, logic is as flexible as a yoga mat, and the act of wearing activewear directly correlates to an increase in fitness levels, irrespective of physical activity. The coefficient of your calorie burn is directly proportional to how snugly your leggings fit.

Imagine that you wake up, workout motivation as absent as socks in a dryer. But then, you pull on leggings and a sports bra. Suddenly, you feel a shift. Your muscles tense in anticipation, and calories start quivering in fear.

By simply wearing activewear, you've tricked your body into thinking it's workout time. Your muscles automatically look for any excuse to tone, and calories start burning away as if you're midway through a marathon, rather than just marathoning episodes of your favorite show. Meanwhile the only thing you're lifting is a cup of coffee to your lips.

Imagine strolling into the grocery store. "Look at her," they'll think, "She must have just run a 5K." Little do they know, your most strenuous activity was choosing between almond or oat milk.

Now, skeptics may argue, "But does it really work?" To which I say, "Does a bear wear activewear in the woods?" The point is, it feels like it works, and in the land of Girl Math, feelings are just as valid as facts.

Rule# 31

The Liquid Diet Loophole

"If my sweet chai tea is so light it doesn't even dent my hunger, it obviously won't make me fat."

—— The Logic ——

If it flows, weight never shows!

According to the sacred scrolls of Girl Math, liquids, regardless of content, are as weightless as your ex's promises. If it's liquid, it basically defies the laws of dietary gravity.

It's Friday night, and you're out with the girls. You've had a salad for dinner because you're "being good," but now you're faced with a cocktail menu. Don't worry, that piña colada isn't a calorie bomb—it's a tropical vacation in a glass. And calories don't count on vacation anyway.

Now, I know what you're thinking: "But what about the sugar? The alcohol? To that, I say, "Shh, we don't hear negativity in the realm of liquid liberty."

This loophole is especially handy for those who view coffee as an essential food group. That caramel macchiato with extra whipped cream? Don't think of it as a dessert; it's your morning fuel. Because in Girl Math, coffee concoctions are a necessity, and necessities shouldn't count against you.

Sometimes, the best thing you can do for your health is to enjoy that glass of wine, savor that latte, and toast to the magic of loopholes. After all, in the grand scheme of things, isn't happiness the true measure of health? So go ahead, raise a glass to the Liquid Diet Loophole, and drink up—the calories don't count here.

Rule# 32

The Workout Duration Delusion

"It's still a two hour workout even if I sat at the juice bar for an hour, because that's healthy too!"

—— The Logic ——

Two hours of the gym counts as a win, no matter how little I spin!

The Workout Duration Delusion bravely ignores such trivial details as actual physical exertion, choosing instead to focus on the paramount importance of gym presence. If you're at the gym longer, you're getting fitter by the minute, right? It's basic math: more time equals more fitness.

The gym is where dreams of a toned physique are forged in the fiery crucible of... well, mostly browsing Instagram between sets. You lift a weight, then rest, checking your phone for what's meant to be a minute—it turns into five. But in the realm of Girl Math, those five minutes are an essential part of the workout. Your muscles are resting, recovering, growing stronger as you double-tap and swipe. It's a ballet of biceps and browsing.

Don't forget the cooldown, an ambiguous period that might involve stretching or sitting on a bench contemplating whether you should have a protein shake. This cooldown is crucial; it's when you plan your triumphant return tomorrow—or maybe after a rest day. Or two.

So, the next time someone asks you how your workout went, just smile and say, "Great! I was there for hours."

Rule# 33

The Comfort Food Exemption

"Wifi is out so I'm stress eating bagel bites. You can talk to me about health when the internet's back."

—— The Logic ——
Emotional eating is tough enough, no need to stress about calorie stuff

Food for emotions doesn't count; food for nutrition does. Now, this might sound like a convenient excuse to raid the pantry after a bad day. But, it's actually a nuanced dietary philosophy that distinguishes between eating our feelings and eating for fuel. The former renders calories powerless, while the latter, well, that's just regular eating with all the boring nutritional accountability.

You've had a bad day, and you're emotionally parched. Suddenly, that pint of ice cream in the freezer is a creamy, dreamy vessel of emotional hydration. As you dive spoon-first into its frosty depths, you're not just indulging in dessert; you're practicing self-care.

Sometimes, the path to feeling better is paved with carbs and sugar, and that's perfectly okay. Our emotional well-being is paramount, and if a slice of pizza (or four) helps us get there, then those slices are as nutritious to our souls as a kale smoothie is to our bodies.

Invoke this rule only in times of need—a breakup, a tough day at work, the season finale of your favorite show, and remember the delicate balance between feeding our bodies and nourishing our souls, for the soul is forever weightless.

Rule # 34

The Unordered Bite Benefit

"He ordered nachos even though I didn't want any, so those few bites I had? Clearly, they're his calories, not mine."

—— The Logic ——

If it's not on my check, it's just a guilt–free peck!

The Unordered Bite Benefit is a principle that miraculously renders any food item calorie-free, provided you weren't the one who ordered it. Yes, you heard it right. If you "weren't hungry" enough to order it, what you do with it after is guilt-free.

Your friend is feeling crazy and orders a chocolate lava cake. It arrives, steaming with chocolaty goodness and a side of vanilla ice cream slowly melting into a puddle of pure joy. You didn't order it, but hey, what's friendship without a little shared dessert? So, you dive in. According to Girl Math, those delicious, molten calories magically evaporate the moment they hit your taste buds. Why? Because it wasn't your order; you're just helping a friend out.

This rule is particularly empowering in the age of shared plates and tapas-style dining. Your friend's French fries? Zero calories. That bite of your sibling's slider? Almost zero calories. It's an act of communal bonding, and no one should be punished for bonding.

Skeptics might argue that this is just a justification for sneaking extra bites without the guilt. Yet, isn't seizing a guilt-free bite you didn't order just making the most out of every moment? The next time you find yourself reaching across the table for a taste of something you didn't order, remember: Girl Math says it's not just allowed; it's encouraged.

Rule# 35

If You Lost Count, Assume More

"Not sure what time I got on the elliptical, but it felt like hours, so that's what I'm telling bae."

—— The Logic ——

Forgot how many? Be an optimist, just add plenty!

Fitness enthusiasts and mathematical mavericks, let's face it, who among us hasn't become so engrossed in our workout playlist that the count of squats or minutes on the treadmill just evaporates into the ether?

Well, when in doubt, always estimate higher. Lost track of your lunges at 12... or was it 13? Congrats, you've done 15. It's called optimistic arithmetic, where every lost count is an opportunity to pat yourself on the back for doing more than you planned.

Imagine you're deep into a set of push-ups, and your focus drifts from "one, two, three..." to "did I remember to text back?" or "what should I binge-watch tonight?" Suddenly, you've no idea if you're on push-up number ten or twenty. This is not a moment of panic but of potential. Let's talk cardio. You're on the elliptical, lost in a daydream or the plot of a podcast, when you realize you've no clue how long you've been pedaling. Was it ten minutes or twenty? It's safe to assume you've been at it for at least half an hour. Your endurance is evidently epic.

Critics might rightfully call this approach delusional. To them, we say, "Isn't optimism the heart of every workout?" It isn't cheating—it's choosing to see the best in your efforts. So, the next time you lose count, remember: in Girl Math, more is always merrier.

Rule# 36

The Vodka Exception

"I swore off drinks to fit my bridesmaid dress, so I'm only doing vodka now."

—— The Logic ——

Vodka's so light, it seems just right!

Welcome to the glittering nightlife of Girl Math, where the beverages sparkle just a little brighter, thanks to almost-zero-calorie vodka. In the enchanting equation of diet logic, vodka isn't just a spirit; it's practically akin to drinking sparkling water.

According to this rule, a vodka soda is a declaration of health-conscious hedonism. You see, vodka is as close to a health potion as you can get. It's clear, it's crisp, and according to our calculations, it's nearly devoid of those pesky caloric critters that lurk in darker liquors. What could it be... 20 calories? 30?

Vodka, in its pure, shimmering essence, is distilled to perfection, leaving behind a beverage so refined, it practically whispers "zero" on the calorie scale. Mix it with soda water, add a squeeze of lime for that vitamin C boost, and voilà — you've got yourself a cocktail that could almost double as a detox drink.

Enjoying a vodka soda is akin to choosing the salad over the fries. It's for the discerning dieter, the gal who wants to let loose without letting go of her wellness goals. So, the next time you're feeling the weight of dietary dilemmas, choose the vodka soda, and sip secure in the knowledge that you're adhering to a sophisticated, scientifically (un)proven health regimen. Here's to your health, your happiness, and Girl Math. Cheers!

Rule# 37

Physical Effort Is Only For Gyms

"Squatted 150 at the gym but asked my boyfriend to pick up the sock I dropped. Gravity's different at home!"

—— The Logic ——

Sweat in the gym is a win, but at home? It's a sin!

There's a little secret we all live by: real exercise only happens in the gym. Outside? Well, that's another story. Carrying groceries or walking across a mammoth parking lot is, like, totally out of the question. "Physical exertion, but at home? That's what boyfriends or husbands are for, right?"

Imagine, just crushing it on the treadmill, feeling like a superhero who could probably run a marathon (or at least daydream about it while scrolling through Insta). But then, the moment someone suggests carrying a slightly heavy shopping bag or—dare I say—taking the stairs instead of the escalator? Suddenly, we're all about conserving energy for the next Zumba class, obviously.

And why? Well, it's like there's this unwritten rule that says only the gym matters and all other forms of exertion are null and void. "Help carry what? Umm, did you not see my epic spin class today? I'm in recovery mode." It's not laziness, per se; it's more about being super strategic about where we invest our energy. Gym energy? Infinite. Real-world energy? Let's not push it.

Why waste precious energy on mundane tasks when it only counts in the gym? After all, in the realm of Girl Math, it all adds up perfectly...as long as we're adding it up on a treadmill.

Rule# 38

Luxury Gyms Are Cheap (Per Use)

"I only go to my unlimited classes once a week, but I could go everyday. Can't beat that value!"

—— The Logic ——
That weekly fee divided by three
is cheap as can be!

So, you've been eyeing that swanky gym membership, the one with its state-of-the-art equipment and those luxurious spa amenities. Maybe I'm talking about the illustrious Equinox, with its $300-a-month price tag that makes your wallet weep just thinking about it. But, it's all about perspective.

If you attend, let's say, 8 classes a month, by the power vested in Girl Math, that breaks down to a mere $37.50 per class. That's not even counting your workouts. Now, if that doesn't sound like a bargain, I don't know what does. A single class at a boutique studio could run you upwards of $30 anyway, and that's without the plush towels and Kombucha on tap!

It's an investment in your health, your happiness, and your right to brag. And let's not forget the social aspect. Where else can you make friends who share your passion for overpriced smoothies and discuss the latest in athleisure trends?

Next time someone questions your high-end gym membership, just dazzle them with your impeccable Girl Math. When you break it down, what seemed like an extravagant expense is actually a cleverly calculated investment. Can you really put a price tag on feeling like a million bucks? Now, let's hit the gym – we've got some luxury sweating to do!

81

Rule# 39

The Treat Termination Tactic

"Eating my heart-shaped chocolates after V-Day is all over? Tragic. Finishing now = a must."

—— The Logic ——
A candy feast today,
keeps tomorrow's cravings at bay!

Uh oh, the house is overrun with sweets, future moments of weakness waiting to pounce. But fear not, for we have devised a master plan so cunning, so daring, it just might work: devour all the sweets now, in one heroic feat, to save our future selves from temptation. Think of it as a tactical dessert strike, eliminating the enemy before it can launch a surprise attack on your unsuspecting willpower.

Imagine a kitchen brimming with chocolates, candies, cakes, oh my! To the untrained eye, it's a paradise. But to us, it's a battlefield, and we're on a mission. Armed with nothing but our forks, we embark on the noble quest of clearing the field. Each bite is not a lapse in self-control; it's a victory against future sugar binges.

By consuming all the sweets in one day, we're actually practicing a form of extreme portion control. Tomorrow, we'll be free from the sugary shackles. Sure, the aftermath might be a sugar coma, and the fleeting thought of "What have I done?" But remember, this is about the long game.

So, the next time you find yourself facing down a battalion of brownies, a legion of lollipops, or a horde of homemade cookies, it's time to take one for the team. With every bite, you're ensuring that future-you won't have to.

Rule# 40

Miniature Munch Maneuver

"I eat my rocky road with a teaspoon, so it's basically calorie-free!"

—— The Logic ——

Any snack is alright,
if your nibbles are light!

You're hit with an unstoppable craving for something sweet. But instead of waving the white flag to temptation, you arm yourself with the smallest spoon in the drawer and begin strolling around your living room between bites. Suddenly, the act of consuming sweets is now a calorie-neutralizing ritual.

By taking tiny bites of your beloved dessert while engaging in a leisurely stroll, you're not actually gaining any weight. Each step taken, each tiny spoonful savored, is part of a strategy to outwit calories. It's a delicate dance of indulgence and movement, where every twirl and tip-toe through the kitchen is a calculated step towards maintaining that sweet balance.

By opting for a miniature spoon, the effort it takes to enjoy your dessert multiplies. And you walk because every step is a silent rebellion against sedentary snacking. It's our way of telling the universe that we can have our cake and eat it too, literally, without the aftermath of guilt. This is not just mindless munching; it's an orchestrated symphony of movement and moderation, a balance so finely tuned that even the most devout dietitian might pause and ponder. So, the next time that dessert whispers your name, remember: tiny bites, endless laps, and the smallest spoon you can find.

Fun Fact:

Although there's health benefits, women who exercise do not lose more weight than women who do not.

What are they going to tell us next, that wearing heels doesn't make us taller?

Source: The Guardian (2010)

Chapter 3:
Paycheck Parables and Budget Balancing Acts

Rule # 41

The Advance Purchase Principle

"Heading to Italy next week, and since I paid last year, it counts as a free trip. Thanks, past me!"

— The Logic —
You'll never feel the sting
if the cost was paid last spring!

If you pay for your trip far enough in advance, by the time you set foot on that plane, you're traveling for free. Although it defies the laws of economics and common sense, it always feels as if the vacation gods have bestowed upon you a complimentary holiday.

The pre-pay strategy is for those who excel at mental gymnastics, turning the pain of today's expense into tomorrow's distant memory. It's a magnificent form of financial amnesia. Never mind that past you might have scrimped, saved, and possibly subsisted on ramen to make it happen. That's a problem for past you, and past you is not on this vacation.

The moment you click 'confirm' on that booking, you're not just reserving a spot on a beach or a room with a view. Oh no, you're locking in happiness at today's price, immune to the inflation of future regret. It's a commitment to future fun, paid with past earnings, enjoyed in the present—a temporal financial paradox that somehow makes perfect sense.

It's a way to trick ourselves into believing we're getting something for nothing, a delightful delusion that enhances the travel experience. So, pack your bags and leave your fiscal responsibility at the departure gate.

Rule# 42

Imaginary Savings Achievements

"Planning to save $50 from my paycheck feels so good, I do it weekly. Actual saving is pending."

—— The Logic ——

You deserve kudos for the saving vibe, even if the dollars don't subscribe!

You're sipping on your overpriced latte, scrolling through lavish vacation rentals, when it hits you—maybe you should start saving some money. So, you spend the next few hours diving deep into blogs about budgeting, nodding along to podcasts on financial freedom, and even adding a budgeting app to your phone. You've not saved a penny, but oh, do you feel accomplished!

It's akin to planning a diet while eating a slice of cake. You know you should be saving money, and you're fully committed to the idea of it. The planning phase is exhilarating; you envision a future where you're financially savvy, with a savings account that's overflowing.

Each thought of saving is accompanied by a mental pat on the back for being so forward-thinking. It's an emotional loophole, a shortcut to feeling financially responsible without the inconvenience of changing your spending habits. After all, in Girl Math, feeling good about your financial plans is half the battle.

Your bank account may never be any fuller, but your heart is. So, here's to the planners, the dreamers, and the someday savers. May your intentions always be as rich as your fantasy bank accounts.

Rule# 43

Venmo Balance is Free Money

"I blew my budget on a dress, so lunch will be on my Venmo balance this week!"

—— The Logic ——

Spending from the Venmo stash hits even less than cash!

Have you ever glanced at your Venmo balance and felt like you'd stumbled upon a windfall? You open the app and money received for your friend's portion of that AirBnB pleasantly surprises you. It's a newfound fortune, ready to be spent with absolute carefree abandon.

It's really great when you're about to make a purchase. There you are, online shopping cart filled, eyeing that checkout button with a mix of excitement and guilt. Then, a light bulb moment: "Wait, I've got money in Venmo!" Suddenly, the guilt dissipates. That balance, accumulated from various ins and outs, now feels like a discount code you didn't know you had. You proceed to checkout, basking in the glow of your savvy financial maneuver.

Why does money, nestled in an app, transform into something that feels, well, free? It's a bit like finding money in a jacket you haven't worn for a season. The truth is, payment apps have turned us all into accidental savers and then into gleeful spenders. We know, deep down, that this money isn't free, yet, the joy of spending it feels different, unburdened by the weight of our bank accounts. So, keep the money in your Venmo balance, because the moment you transfer back to your bank account, the magic is gone.

93

Rule# 44

Always Blame the Economy

"Checked my bank statement and it's not looking great. I really hope the economy picks up."

—— The Logic ——

If I have money, it's cuz of me, if I don't, it's the economy!

When in doubt, blame the economy. Not just any economy, but an elusive, omnipotent entity that seems to specifically target your financial well-being. This rule is a one-size-fits-all solution to life's financial quandaries.

Struggling to pay rent on your apartment? It's not because you splurged on that artisanal coffee maker; rents are simply too astronomical. And why are rents high? The economy, of course! Job market got you down? Can't find employment that values your degree in underwater basket weaving? The unemployment rate is just too darn high. Is your retirement account not even enough to pay for Netflix in your golden years? Well, why save for retirement when inflation is lurking around the corner? It's the rational response to an economy where today's dollar is tomorrow's penny.

Conversations at parties, once dominated by humblebrags about promotions, have now evolved into competitive lamentations. "You think your rent's high? Let me tell you about my renewal offer!"

In sum, when life gives you lemons, don't make lemonade—that requires sugar and effort. Instead, blame the economy. It's a no-fail, guilt-free way to navigate the choppy waters of personal finance.

Rule# 45

The Surplus Splurge Statute

"Every time I finish paying bills and see leftover money, my inner voice says 'concert tickets'."

—— The Logic ——

After expenses are cleared, the fun is here!

There's a golden rule that shines brighter than a clearance sale at your favorite store: "Once the bills are paid, every penny left is dubbed fun money." It's basically a mantra for the financially savvy. You've just finished adulting so hard, paying all those grown-up bills. Rent? Done. Electricity? Covered. Internet? Sorted. And there, in the glowing light of your banking app, sits a little pile of money. It's not earmarked for anything responsible. Oh no, this money has a higher calling: pure, unadulterated fun.

This is a reward, a treasure trove of joy waiting to be unleashed on anything that screams happiness. A new pair of shoes that you definitely need? Absolutely. Dinner at that fancy new spot downtown? Count me in. In the world of Girl Math, this leftover money is a magical fund that doesn't adhere to the usual financial laws. It multiplies joy and subtracts worries. It's proof that you're doing life right. After all, what's the point of working so hard if you can't enjoy the fruits of your labor in the form of a spontaneous shopping spree or a gourmet feast?

So, the next time you find yourself with some "extra" cash after the bills are paid, remember this sacred rule. It's not just leftover money; it's your well-earned ticket to happiness.

Rule# 46

The Per-Use Paradox

"I realized my luxury watch is a bargain if you consider I check the time like, 100 times a day."

—— The Logic ——

If you want to see your guilt reduce, divide the price by each use!

In the fabulous world of Girl Math, there exists a magical formula that can turn even the most eye-watering expenses into what seems like mere pocket change. It's like finding a cheat code in the game of shopping.

Picture this: a pair of designer boots that cost a hefty $200. Enter the wizardry of Girl Math. If those boots are worn for 100 days of winter bliss, we're talking $2 per wear. Don't even get me started on that espresso machine eyeballing you from your wishlist. Say it's $300, and it brews a heavenly cup every morning for a year. That's roughly 82 cents per cup. Take that, overpriced coffee shop!

As we navigate the shopping spree circus, filled with temptations at every turn, this rule lights the way like a dazzling disco ball, reminding you of the joy (and low cost) each use brings.

So, when that divine piece calls out to you, casting a shadow of doubt with its steep cost, whip out your Girl Math calculator. Break it down, laugh in the face of buyer's remorse. Because, with Girl Math, it's not about the price—it's about how fabulously frugal you feel with each wear, sip, or carry.

Rule# 47

The Work Expense Loophole

"My Airpods Pro upgrade was guilt-free because I use them for work calls!"

—— The Logic ——

If it helps me make money, it's free, honey!

This rule is simple. If it makes the 9-to-5 glide by, it's not an expense, it is literally paying for itself. Consider the power of the work wardrobe. That sharply tailored blazer is not just fabric and buttons; it's sophistication armor. When you strut into the office or that Zoom call, every dollar spent on those threads is earning its keep.

And let's talk about the magical midday elixir known as the latte. Some say it's just coffee; we say it's liquid motivation. Each sip propels you through the afternoon slump. That $5 spent daily? It's the fuel for your financial fire, because let's face it, those reports aren't going to file themselves.

Your happy hour drinks with colleagues are a bonding experience, a strategic alliance formed over discounted appetizers and shared laughter. Each delicious margarita is a round invested in your social capital.

Now, for those skeptics lurking in the shadows, murmuring about budgets and frivolous spending, let's be clear: in the grand ledger of life, if it brings a smile to your face and a skip to your step in the daily grind, it's not an expense. It's a dividend-paying stock in your personal happiness and professional growth portfolio. Equipped with some Girl Math, every purchase can be a pathway to prosperity.

Rule # 48

Tax Returns Are Fun Money

"The $200 I spent on shoes was less than my tax refund, so it's totally okay!"

—— The Logic ——

You can spend tax returns without fear, if you just forget it was yours all year!

Ah, Tax Return Season, that time of year when the government, in a rare display of generosity, decides to give back a slice of what we've painstakingly contributed over the past year. It's the universe rewarding you for all those hours spent in fluorescent-lit offices, for braving the commute, and for all the times you used that awful office restroom. This is your bonus for enduring adulthood.

Now, some might say, "Invest it wisely. Save for a rainy day." But we see it differently. This is a golden opportunity to infuse joy into our otherwise meticulously budgeted lives. Wink, wink!

So, what does one do with this fun fund? A splurge at the spa, perhaps. Or maybe it's time for that designer bag you've been eyeing, whispering to you every time you open Instagram. It could even be a spontaneous weekend getaway. Let's not forget the joy of shopping sprees, where every purchase is a high-five to oneself for navigating TurboTax.

In conclusion, while the world tells you it was your money all along, Girl Math invites you to treat it like a windfall. Life isn't just about making ends meet; it's about making memories. And if a fake windfall from the taxman can create those moments of joy, then by all means, let the fun begin.

Rule# 49
The Subscription Shrug-off

"Oops, wine club renewed by itself again. I didn't even notice until the box arrived. Oh well, cheers to me!"

—— The Logic ——

If I didn't click buy, no need to justify!

If a charge happens automatically, can we really be blamed for it? I mean really, if I don't manually click "buy," is it truly a splurge?

You're sifting through your bank statement, and whoops, there it is—another month of that gourmet cheese club subscription. You joined during an adventurous and wine-fueled evening. But hey, it's automatic, so technically, the universe made that decision, not you. And then there's the gym membership. January you was all about that "new year, new me" life. Now, not so much. But those automatic withdrawals? Not your fault. You're just a victim of your past self's optimism.

Let's not forget the app subscriptions and streaming services. You downloaded that meditation app with the best of intentions. Yet, somehow, finding inner peace slipped your mind, but the app didn't forget about you. It lovingly takes its monthly toll on your bank account. Like how you signed up to watch that one show everyone's been talking about, and now you're six streaming services deep.

If we had to consciously choose each of these expenses every month, think of all the stuff we'd miss out on. Maybe one day, you'll actually use all those subscriptions. Or not. Either way, it's not really your fault.

Rule # 50
The Payroll Deduction Delight

"Payroll-deducted vision insurance got me Gucci shades, which means... they free, baby!"

—— The Logic ——

If it skips my bank, the costs don't spank!

Pre-tax deductions are money that evaporates before it lands in your bank account, effectively making any associated expenses feel like they're happening in an alternate universe.

From healthcare premiums to retirement savings, these amounts are spirited away before you even get a whiff of your salary. Since you never get to hold this money, spending it doesn't quite register in your brain as actual spending. This Girl Math sorcery relies heavily on the "ignorance is bliss" philosophy. If the money never makes it to your checking account, is it really gone? Instead of consciously and manually setting aside funds for dreary things like dental plans or 401(k)s, the pre-tax magic does it for you, all while allowing you to live in the happy delusion you don't really have a choice.

It's denial in its best form, and it's actually good for you this time. But the best part is that it dulls the guilt when you spend the rest of your paycheck, because the important stuff was already paid for, right? Who knew fiscal responsibility could be so effortless?

So, the next time you grumble about your net income, remember the pre-tax enchantments at work. These deductions are not just disappearing acts but investments in your future happiness and health, cleverly disguised as financial vanishing tricks. **107**

Rule# 51

Always Round Down

"GPS says I'm 19 minutes away from the restaurant, so I told my friends I'm 15 minutes out."

—— The Logic ——

Shave off a few, it's what we do!

You're eyeing that gorgeous dress, the one that's been calling your name every time you walk past the store. The price? $149.99. In Girl Math land, that extra penny off does wonders—you're allowed to register it as basically $100. And well, that's a green light to the "why not?" One penny more and the cost would have been prohibitive. It's not about the amount you spend; it's about the amount you think you're spending.

The beauty of this rule lies in its flexibility. It applies to everything from prices to times to counting. Planning to leave at 7:30 and got out the door at 7:52? Congrats, you're on time!

Be proud of yourself, because rounding down is a testament to your optimistic side. Nevermind the rationale, which is as solid as it is utterly, delightfully dubious.

In conclusion, this rule isn't just a part of Girl Math; it's a cornerstone of our philosophy that we'll never really understand, and that's okay. It's a rule that whispers sweet nothings of leniency into our ears, allowing us to bask in the glory of our own cleverness. So, the next time you're faced with a $29.99 price tag, remember: in Girl Math, that's practically $20. And who can argue with that?

Rule # 52
Just Trying to Budget
Is Good Enough

"I've got a budget app, so I'm officially adulting. Using it is the next level."

—— The Logic ——
A budget app is a thrill
even if you download and chill!

Snagging a budgeting app is like a front-row seat to financial wisdom—except, you know, without actually attending the show. It promises riches and responsibility with a mere tap.

"Got my budgeting app; I'm basically a finance guru now," you proclaim, sipping on that extra foam latte you categorized under "essential self-care expenses." The app, your shiny beacon of hope in a sea of receipts, is more of a trophy than a tool. It's like buying gym clothes for the fitness vibe without ever planning to sweat.

The first few days post-download are a honeymoon phase. You track expenses like a detective, every coffee purchase a clue to your monetary habits. But as enthusiasm wanes, the app's reminders morph from helpful nudges to nagging in-laws. Suddenly, checking it feels like opening a fridge full of healthy food when you're craving pizza.

Yet, in the logic of Girl Math, merely possessing the app is akin to having your financial act together. It's a comforting illusion. "I might not follow it, but hey, it's there." In essence, while the app's notifications fade into the background, your financial savviness shines. Because in Girl Math, it's not the budgeting that counts, but the boldness of the attempt.

Rule# 53
Partner Purchasing Equality

"I couldn't believe what he paid for a golf membership, so I splurged on a spa weekend. Balance restored!"

—— The Logic ——

When a new toy brings him glee, it's my turn for a shopping spree!

If your significant other has recently indulged in a wallet-weeping purchase, it's not just your right, but your solemn duty, to outspend them in a glorious display of monetary might.

Next time your quiet evening is disrupted by the arrival of a new golf set, accompanied by the obnoxious gleeful pride of your partner, panic not, for Girl Math is on your side. This isn't a moment of fiscal fear; it's a golden ticket to your own spending spree. It's now your obligation to achieve that perfect balance in the relationship ledger where each penny spent by your partner is met with equal (or greater) spending by you. Hey, it's healthier than getting angry!

This isn't about revenge; it's about harmony. Critics may call it petty; accountants may deem it financially unfeasible; but it's maintaining the equilibrium. However, beware the spiral, for this path is fraught with overdraft fees. The key is not just to spend more, but to spend smarter. Your partner bought a new gaming console? Time for that designer handbag that doubles as an "investment. " That is, an investment in the principles of fairness, equity, and slightly passive-aggressive love. After all, love isn't just about sharing a life, it's about sharing a perfectly justified, mutually assured splurge.

Rule # 55

Budgets Are Meant to be Stretched

"Count me in for Lollapalooza... Budgets, schmudgets!"

—— The Logic ——
A budget's a goal, not a limit, go over? There's no sin in it!

In the sparkly universe of Girl Math, budgets are more like suggestions. Think of your budget as a stretchy yoga pant – it can handle a little extra! So, you went a tad overboard at that sale? That's not splurging; it's just your budget doing some yoga stretches.

Every "Sale" sign is essentially the universe winking at you, saying, "Girl, stretch that budget a bit more." That extra pair of boots? It's not an expense; it's an extension of your budget's flexibility. And who are we to argue with the universe?

Think of it this way: If budgets were rigid, how would we ever fit in those emergency shopping sprees or those "just because" treats? Like, if I skip my morning latte for a week, I've basically earned that sparkly phone case, right? It's simple Girl Math – subtract here, add there, and voilà, guilt-free shopping!

And for those moments when you feel a pinch of buyer's remorse? Just remember there's a reason the word "overbudget" exists. Next time you're wincing at the checkout, just remind yourself: "A stretched budget is a happy budget." Life's too short for rigid limits.

Rule# 56

The Ignorance Is Bliss Rule

"I treat my accounts like a horror flick; I cover my eyes during the scary parts!"

—— The Logic ——

If you don't peek, it's not bleak!

Ignorance isn't just bliss; it's strategic. Last night's shopping spree? A figment of your imagination unless you dare to check your account. Money running low? An urban legend, until you break and log in. Student loans reaching astronomical heights? In this dimension, they're just numbers floating in the ether.

This principle extends into every facet of your financial life. Overdraft fees become mere whispers on the wind, credit card statements transform into ancient hieroglyphics. It's selective financial attention, a crucial skill in the arsenal of any seasoned Girl Math practitioner.

The act of not checking your balance requires grace, a pinch of delusion, and a steadfast commitment to the mantra, "What I don't know can't hurt me." Each unopened statement is a step in the ballet of blissful ignorance. But beware, a peek behind the curtain, a glance at your balance, and the magic dissipates, leaving you face to face with the cold, hard digits of reality. Yet, fear not, for as long as there are unopened emails and unlogged apps, the fantasy can be reborn.

So, the next time financial accountability looms, remember the sacred scrolls of Girl Math: "Let the numbers haunt someone else's dreams."

Rule# 57

Financial Future Optimism

"I'll never marry rich if I don't start living like I am already!"

—— The Logic ——

Buy now with zeal, future wealth is real!

Future you is definitely hitting the jackpot. Maybe it's that degree you're working on, the pending promotion, or those millions of followers just waiting to discover your social media. Whichever it is, you're on a one-way trip to Successville.

So if you're eyeing that 5 star hotel for your next getaway with a price tag that is eye-watering, remember in the grand scheme of things, it's just a drop in the ocean of your future wealth. You're going to make it big, so what's a little splurge on the way up? Every purchase now is an advance on your inevitable wealth. That fancy dinner, those concert tickets, the high-end gadgets—it's all just practice for when you're swimming in cash. Think of it as acclimating to the high life.

If there's any naysayers, they're just not visionaries like you. They can't see the empire you're building, as soon as you have a great idea! So, the next time you splurge a little, remember: it's all part of the plan. Future you is grateful for the head start on living lavishly.

If the path to riches is paved with a few too many online shopping packages… well, that's just the scenic route. So go ahead, live a little today – future you has got the tab.

Rule# 58

Windfalls Are For YOLOing

"Hit a jackpot on a slot machine, time for some bottle service, baby! My student loan debt can wait."

—— The Logic ——

If it was easy to earn, it's easy to burn!

You're strolling through life, minding your own business, when out of the blue, you receive an unexpected windfall—a stock certificate for Amazon, gifted by a long-lost relative. It's like finding a winning lottery ticket in a discarded magazine— utterly surprising and oh-so exhilarating!

Now, armed with this unexpected wealth, you feel like a modern-day Rockefeller, ready to conquer the world one impulsive purchase at a time. That luxury watch you've been eyeing? Consider it yours! And those front-row tickets to the hottest Broadway show? Snatch 'em up before they're gone! After all, unexpected money feels like a VIP pass to the land of indulgence.

Forget about mundane responsibilities like your towering student loan debt or those nagging credit card bills. Who needs financial prudence when you have a golden ticket to financial freedom, right? So what if your car desperately needs a brake job or your kitchen appliances are on the fritz? There's plenty of time for practicalities later!

However, before you go on a spending spree of epic proportions, reality taps you on the shoulder. Let's just say Uncle Sam isn't as forgiving as your whimsical dreams.

Rule # 59

The Happiness Quotient

"I know $800 for Adele tickets sounds insane, but if you knew how happy it made me, you'd totally get it!"

—— The Logic ——

It's good money spent, if the soul's content!

Spending equals happiness, and the value of the spend is best measured in how happy it makes you. That's right—happiness is just a swipe away, like a magician pulling joy out of a top hat or, in this case, a wallet!

Some say true happiness comes from deep connections and inner peace, but who needs that when you've got the latest fashion trends and brunch selfies to fuel your Insta fame? And who needs savings accounts when your closet's bursting at the seams with designer labels and your pantry's stocked with artisanal chocolates? Financial security sounds great, but have you ever experienced the sheer ecstasy of unboxing a delivery from your favorite online retailer? It's like Christmas morning!

Feeling blue? Buy something shiny. Stressed out? Spa day, stat! Existential crisis? Nothing a little indulgence can't fix—or at least distract you from momentarily!

So, splurge my loves, and remember that while the best things in life are often free—like laughter, love, and the occasional cat video, you can only watch it if you have the latest iPhone. May your days be filled with joy, laughter, and just the right amount of retail therapy.

Rule# 60

Sooner is Always Better

"Paris-bound because I've got a rendezvous with destiny, and she's not a patient woman!"

—— The Logic ——

She who jumps the gun has all the fun!

Sooner is always better! Yes, why wait when you can pounce now and milk it for all it's worth? Imagine this: you're eyeing that dream "forever" home, and the price tag is staring you down like a ferocious beast. Everyone else is saying go for that "starter home," but they don't realize that buying your forever home now means getting more value out of it in the long run.

And what about those everyday essentials? Take that sleek new smartphone, for instance. Sure, it may cost an arm and a leg upfront, but it's literally losing value everyday you don't buy it as it inches closer towards obsolescence. From state-of-the-art appliances to futuristic furniture, every purchase promises a world of convenience and comfort that you should be deriving value from right now.

However, my fellow dreamers, before you gallop off into the sunset in a frenzy of hasty purchases, let me sprinkle a dash of reality on your rainbow-colored dreams. While it's true that seizing the moment can lead to extraordinary experiences and instant gratification, true wisdom lies in balancing impulsivity with prudence. Trust me, you don't want to be stuck mowing an endless expanse of lawn on your "forever home," only to realize that you'd be happier with a tiny home and a hammock!

Fun Fact:

On average, female investors achieve more returns than males by 40 basis points, possibly due to less risk-taking.

We save our risk-taking for cutting our own bangs.

Source: CNBC (2021)

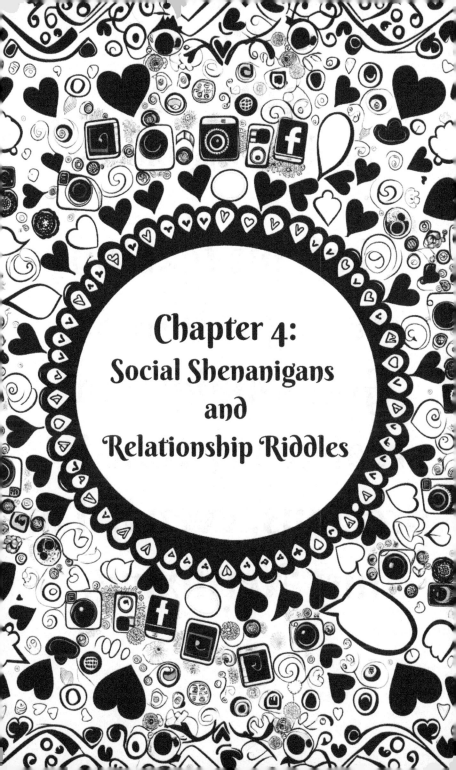

Chapter 4:
Social Shenanigans
and
Relationship Riddles

Rule# 61

The Reply Delay Dividend

"Left his text 'on read' for hours. Gotta make him realize my time is precious, even if I'm just Netflixing."

—— The Logic ——

If you wait a beat, you build your mystique!

Here's the deal: the longer you take to reply, the more social cred you earn. It's like playing hard to get, but for all your convos—dating, friends, work, you name it!

You're texting your crush, and they hit you with a "wyd." If you fire back immediately, you're basically screaming, "I'm desperate and available for you 24/7!" But if you wait a beat before hitting send, suddenly you're mysterious. And let's be real, who doesn't want to be a little mysterious? So, next time you're tempted to reply right away, take a sec to let that message marinate, and watch as your social stock skyrockets.

And it's not just for dating drama—it works for all your convos. Replying too quickly to your BFF's text? Won't be BFF for long! Same goes for work stuff. Replying to emails at lightning speed? Sure, it shows you're on top of things, but it also screams, "I have nothing else going on!" Take a breath, let that email sit for a bit, and watch as your boss starts treating you like the CEO you are.

So there you have it, the secret to texting success is simple—delayed replies are your new best friend. So embrace the art of the wait, and get ready to level up your social game like never before!

Rule# 62

Date Night Mathematics

"He ordered us the lobster? Looks like I've just upgraded my relationship status to 'getting serious'!"

— The Logic —

If he drops some dough, your love will glow!

The fancier the restaurant, the deeper the depths of your relationship! It's like decoding a secret message written in the language of appetizers and entrees.

You're seated at a candlelit table, surrounded by elegant ambiance. Every choice becomes a clue to the mysteries of your budding romance. Will he opt for the humble burger, signaling a laid-back approach to love? Or will he go for the extravagant steak, hinting at a desire for something more substantial?

And let's not forget the drinks—oh no, my fellow gastronomical detectives, for every sip tells a story. Is he a beer kind of guy, content with life's simple pleasures? Or does he reach for the sophisticated Manhattan, signaling a taste for the finer things in life—and perhaps, in love?

But here's the twist, while Date Night Mathematics may seem like a foolproof formula for decoding romance, sometimes, the simplest meals shared with the right person can be more meaningful than any Michelin-starred extravaganza. So, whether your date orders the burger or the steak, the beer or the Manhattan, remember while the order may be a clue, it's mostly about the laughter shared, the stories told, and the warmth of a genuine connection, served with a side of fries and a sprinkle of laughter.

Rule# 63

The Favor Formula

"I let her borrow my fave dress, now she's contractually obligated to like all my Instagram posts."

—— The Logic ——

If you boost their vibe, they'll help you thrive!

Every act of kindness earns you coveted friendship points, redeemable for favors! It's like building up your Sim's friendship bar. Listened to your friend's drama for 20 minutes? Now she has to pretend to enjoy the memes you're going to send her later!

Imagine this: you're on a mission to solidify your status as the ultimate gal pal by showcasing your generosity, so you offer to pick up your BFF's daily dose of caffeine from Starbucks. But it's not just about coffee runs—oh no, it's about racking up those points for future favor redemption.

As you strut into Starbucks, you can practically feel the friendship points stacking up with each step. You confidently place the order and, for good measure, toss in an extra pack of mints because who doesn't love a bonus favor? Returning to your squad with coffee in hand, you can't help but revel in the glory of your newfound friendship points. "I got this round, babe," you announce proudly.

As the days pass, you eagerly anticipate cashing in on your Starbucks run favor. You know that when the time comes for you to belt out a cringe-worthy rendition of "Bad Romance" at karaoke night, your BFF will be there, front and center, serving as your ultimate hype squad—cheering you on through every off-key note and dramatic hair flip.

Rule# 64

The Ghosting Paradox

"I ghosted him last week, but he hasn't messaged me since. What the actual hell?"

—— The Logic ——

No clue why you're single while you ghost every pringle!

Ghosting reigns supreme as the ultimate mystery of the digital age. Let's dive into the enigma—it's part probability theory, part love story, and all hilarity.

Imagine you're navigating the treacherous waters of online dating, armed with your wits and a smartphone. You strike up a conversation with a potential love interest, and for a moment, sparks fly. But soon, the conversation fizzles out into the abyss of unread messages and unanswered emojis.

You see, when you stop texting, it's like subtracting yourself from the equation and waiting to see if the other person somehow solves for 'x'—and spoiler alert, 'x' is you! For every ghosting, you still think there's a chance of a love-struck return.

Now, you might be thinking, "How could you ever find love if you ghost everyone?" Ah, but therein lies the beauty of the Ghosting Probability Paradox—it's a paradox within a paradox, a conundrum wrapped in a riddle, where the rules of etiquette are as fluid as a love-drunk confession at 2 a.m.

So, the next time you find yourself in the throes of a ghosting dilemma, instead of going radio silent, maybe roll the dice, play the odds, and above all else, embrace the whimsical chaos of modern romance. **135**

Rule# 65

The Birthday Memory Coefficient

"I was low-key sus about Sarah, but she texted at midnight on my birthday, so now she's squad material."

—— The Logic ——

You know that friendship slay if they memorize your birthday!

An essential concept in Girl Math that determines the depth of social bonds is the simple act of remembering someone's birthday without the aid of digital reminders. It's akin to solving a complex equation without a calculator, elevating your friendship status to a higher echelon.

Recalling a birthday without digital nudges isn't just impressive; it's a superpower. It signifies that your bond transcends the superficiality of virtual reminders. Sure, anyone can send a generic "HBD" message after being reminded by Facebook, but to recall the date without digital nudges? Now, that's the stuff of legend.

Mastering this art isn't without its rewards. From the warm glow of appreciation to the social brownie points accumulated, the benefits are abundant. But beware the flip side—forgetting a birthday can lead to a social faux pas of epic proportions.

In conclusion, the Birthday Memory Coefficient is the most straightforward testament to the strength of your friendships. So, embrace the challenge, sharpen your memory, and watch as your bonds grow stronger with each heartfelt birthday wish. After all, in the equation of life, genuine gestures count far more than digital reminders.

Rule# 66

The Social Media Story Slope

"Got into a wreck today. Can't wait to post about it. Just gotta figure out how much I can milk it!"

—— The Logic ——

Post more razzle and enjoy more dazzle!

Social media posting is crafting a narrative that's part reality, part fantasy, and all perfectly filtered, and story posts beckon you immerse yourself in someone else's curated reality. Each swipe is like a step up the engagement ladder. But beware, my friends, for with great engagement comes great responsibility... and perhaps a touch of digital fatigue.

Now, let's delve into the mathematics of it all. Think of your story posts as points plotted on the graph of your digital life. The more frequent the posts, the steeper the slope of your engagement curve. Just like in algebra class, every post is like a coefficient in an equation, incrementally increasing the perceived excitement of your daily saga.

Of course, there's a delicate balance to maintain. Too few posts, and you risk fading into the digital abyss, lost among the sea of selfies and sunset shots. Too many posts, and you run the risk of overwhelming your followers with an onslaught of updates, like a never-ending stream of consciousness in their feed.

Finding that sweet spot on the engagement curve is an art form in itself. It's about the perfect balance between quantity and quality, between authenticity and aesthetics. So go forth, and may your social stories be as captivating as they are calculated.

Rule# 67

Texting is Always More Efficient

"Mom's angry, so I'm skipping her call. Doesn't she know emojis are better than words?"

—— The Logic ——

Calling is a drag, texting is my swag!

Twenty minutes of texting is always more efficient than a two-minute phone call. Imagine your phone lights up with a notification—a call from Becky. Oh right, she wants you to grab a cake for the party.

You pause and contemplatie the options. On one hand, you could engage in a quick phone call with Becky, exchanging pleasantries and learning what kind of cake. But wait! Efficiency is key. Why go through the hassle of a 2 minute call when you could embark on a text-based journey lasting 20 minutes or more about what flavor to get, what size, what kind of ice cream, if plastic bowls are needed, etc, etc?

With a flick of your thumb, you open your messaging app and begin crafting the perfect response. "Sorry, can't talk, BF is sleeping." Before you know it, you've delved into a texting logistical blackhole.

But let's not forget the most crucial aspect of this Girl Math rule: the art of multitasking. While engaged in a lively text exchange, you can simultaneously binge-watch your favorite TV show or whip up a gourmet meal—all without missing a beat.

So, the next time you find yourself faced with the age-old dilemma of texting versus calling, remember the golden rule of Girl Math: when it comes to efficiency, texting always takes the crown. **141**

Rule # 68

25 Is So Old/Young!

"Can't believe 25 is halfway to 50. I guess I can give up on the Hogwartz letter."

—— The Logic ——

25's ancient when you're a tot,
but young when you're a seasoned thot!

When we're young, we envision our future selves as these accomplished adults who have it all together by the time they hit the ripe old age of 25. We imagine having a Pinterest-worthy home and balancing work, relationships, and self-care. But oh, how reality loves to throw us a curveball!

As the years tick by and the dreaded 25 approaches, suddenly, the prospect of being a quarter-century old feels daunting. We make pacts with friends, jokingly agreeing to marry each other if we're still single at 25, as if life is over after that. But then, the big day arrives, and guess what? We're still just as clueless as we were at 18, except now we have bills to pay and constant existential dread.

Fast forward, and here we are, standing on the precipice of our thirties. Oh, how we long for the days when 25 felt ancient and 30 seemed like a distant speck on the horizon! We'd give anything to go back to when the biggest stress was figuring out how to operate a laundry machine.

Maybe someday, when you're sipping champagne on your yacht in the south of France, you'll look back on your thirties with a fondness you never knew possible, realizing that the best years of your life were just beginning.

Rule# 69

Old Friendships Have More Value

"Sure, Sarah's been a bitch recently, but I've known her since 1st grade so of course I'll be her bridesmaid!"

—— The Logic ——
Old friends are like vintage wine, even if they're kinda asinine!

The equation of friendship has its own unique set of variables. It's not just about compatibility or shared interests; it's about the sheer duration of the bond, regardless of its flaws. Think about your oldest childhood friend, inseparable since the days of birthday parties at Chuck E. Cheese, navigating the ups and downs of life together. Sure, they may have their quirks and imperfections, but their presence in your life is like an anchor in a sea of uncertainty.

Now, contrast that with a new friend, someone who seems perfect on the surface – charming, witty, and always up for an adventure. But beneath the shiny exterior lies a void where the shared history and deep-rooted connection of a lifelong friendship should be. It's like trying to compare a priceless antique with a shiny new bauble – sure, the bauble may catch your eye, but it lacks the depth and richness of history that makes the antique truly special.

The Girl Math principle at play here is that the longer you've been friends with someone, the more value they have to you regardless of what they actually have to offer. So, always remember: it's not about finding the perfect friend; it's about cherishing the imperfect ones who have stood by your side through thick and thin.

Rule# 70

Only Swiping Left is Still Dating

"When I'm down about being single, I fire up Tinder, swipe left, and instantly feel better about myself!"

—— The Logic ——
Swiping left—only,
filters out the baloney!

The pursuit of love often feels like a never-ending game of digital roulette. But fear not, my fellow swipers, for in the midst of this whirlwind of heart emojis and profile pics, there exists a hidden gem of Girl Math wisdom: the paradox of left-only swiping.

You're nestled cozily on your couch, phone in hand, ready to dive into your potential matches. With each swipe, you feel a sense of accomplishment, eliminating bad apples after bad apples. Left, left, left. And yet, amidst the sea of rejected profiles and missed connections, you can't help but feel a smug reassurance that you're doing something right.

It's a subconscious belief that by swiping left on every profile that crosses your path, you're somehow increasing your chances of finding true love. It's like trying to win the lottery by never buying a ticket. And yet, here we are, boldly embracing the contradiction, convinced that our unwavering commitment to the left swipe will eventually lead us to our happily ever after.

To all the skeptics and naysayers who scoff at our unconventional approach to online dating, we say this: don't knock it till you've tried it. What's better than feeling like you're trying your best to find the one without actually having to stress about dates? **147**

Rule# 71

More Emojis Means More Vibes

"Using 10 laughing-crying emojis makes my joke 10 times funnier, right?"

—— The Logic ——

Emoji parades make the excitement cascade!

Girl math dictates that the more emojis you use, the bigger the excitement! Next time you need to fake being thrilled about something, send a message with a flurry of excited emojis, accompanied by a thumbs-up and a dancing lady. Girl math says that more emojis can turn any muted emotions into perceived excitement!

It's great for genuine excitement too! Let's say your boyfriend texts you with the news that he's finally agreed to get a puppy. Your heart skips a beat with excitement, so you unleash a barrage of puppy emojis—paw prints, dog faces, and even a little bone thrown in for good measure. Now the boyfriend feels like man of the year.

Emojis are also a handy tool for deciphering emotions. You're not sure your friend had a good time on her Tinder date, after she only said, "It was good." Then, you notice a string of heart-eyed emojis at the end of her message, and suddenly, everything becomes clear. She's head over heels, and it's time to break out the champagne and celebrate her newfound romance!

Emojis reign supreme as the ultimate expression of excitement, enthusiasm, and everything in between. So, remember: when in doubt, add more emojis!

Rule# 72

The Closure Text

"I know I shouldn't text him, but he really should know that my cat still misses him more than I do."

—— The Logic ——

Texting for closure is just emotional exposure!

Texting an ex for 'closure' is a bit like trying to balance your emotional checkbook. It seems straightforward – a quick message for a neat sum-up. But often, this move adds more questions than answers, turning what you thought was a simple tally into a complex calculus of 'what-ifs' and 'maybes.' It's like a risky math problem where you aim for zero but might just end up doubling the emotional investment!

You're nestled on your couch, surrounded by a fortress of tissues and half-finished tubs of ice cream. Suddenly, it hits you – why not just shoot your ex a text? Closure seems just a send button away, right? Wrong. Enter the turmoil of closure-seeking, where the simple act of hitting send on that carefully composed message unleashes a storm of emotions – nostalgia, regret, and perhaps even a hint of longing.

Amidst the chaos, there's the absurdity of convincing yourself that sending a Snapchat instead of a text somehow makes the closure process less intense. And let's not forget consulting a horoscope or psychic hotline to determine the best time to send the closure text for maximum cosmic alignment. The moral of the story? Proceed with caution. After all, in the whimsical world of Girl Math, sometimes it's better to let sleeping dogs lie and focus on forging ahead, one clumsy step at a time.

Rule# 73

Party Invitations Boost Your Ego

"When asked if I have plans this week, I casually drop I have five party invites... but who's counting? Oh right, me!"

— The Logic —

It's always a delight to feel like a socialite!

You find yourself lounging at home on a Saturday night, contemplating the state of your social calendar—or lack thereof. With each passing minute of scrolling through your phone, the absence of party invites starts to weigh on you. It's as if the universe has forgotten your existence, leaving you to ponder whether your popularity has hit rock bottom.

Fast forward two months, and suddenly, your inbox is inundated with a flurry of party invitations. Friendsgivings, housewarmings, game nights—you name it, and you've got an invite for it. You feel great—why does everyone love me so much?!

Navigating this whirlwind of social engagements, you can't help but chuckle at the peculiar arithmetic of popularity. The more party invites flood your inbox, the higher you feel your status soars. It's Girl Math's quirky reminder that sometimes, popularity is just a numbers game.

Yet, amidst this amusing chaos, you ponder the absurdity of it all. You know deep down that your worth isn't measured by the number of invites you snag. But let's face it, there's an undeniable rush that comes with each ping of a new party invite. Nevermind how many game night dud's you attend, or goldfish birthday parties, popular is popular!

Rule# 74

The Meme-Share Metric

"Haven't seen Suzie in months, but I know we're tight cuz she sends me daily memes on 'the gram'!"

—— The Logic ——

Our friendship won't flop if humor we swap!

The more memes you're itching to share with someone, the closer they are to being your BFF! It's like the new version of those best friend bracelets from middle school. Instead of wearing matching jewelry, you're now connecting through the power of internet humor. Each time you share a hilarious meme, it's like adding another sparkly bead to your friendship chain. But the real magic happens when your friend reciprocates. It's like they're saying, "Hey, you're not just my friend; you're my meme soulmate."

Of course, there's an art to meme sharing. You have to know your friend's sense of humor inside and out. You can't just send them any old meme and expect it to stick. No, it has to be the perfect combination of relatable, hilarious, and a little bit absurd. And let's not forget the thrill of seeing that notification pop up on your phone: "[Friend] shared a post with you."

But beware, not all meme sharing is created equal. There's a fine line between being the cool meme-sharing friend and the annoying oversharer. You have to strike the right balance between sharing funny content and overwhelming your friends with notifications, or they may lowkey mute you. Also, never share more than like, two or three memes until you get one back, or you give ick vibes. Afterall, sharing a meme is like sending a digital hug wrapped in humor.

Rule# 75

The Gift-Giving Gauge

"When Sarah got me a toaster, I realized our friendship might be toast."

—— The Logic ——

The size of a gift can make a friendship shift!

We've all been there, unintentionally evaluating our friendships based on the size of the gifts we receive. We're just hardwired to equate the value of the present with the worth of the person giving it. A crappy friend gives crappy gifts (relative to their income), right? You peel back the wrapping paper to reveal a pack of dollar store stickers, you can't help but think, "Well, that's Brenda for you."

But when we're the ones doing the giving, suddenly, the size of the gift isn't about how good a friend we are – it's about how much money and effort they were worth. Don't those thrift store cat socks look perfect for thrifty Brenda?

Gifts have a way of taking you on a social rollercoaster. Like when your coworker surprises you with a thoughtful homemade treat, and you find yourself reevaluating your perception of them. Or when your bestie hands you a gift-wrapped box, and inside is a Scooby Doo T-shirt, leaving you questioning not only your friendship but her fashion sense as well!

Remember the intricate dance of cognitive dissonance at play. Whether giving or receiving, if the gift falls flat, it's on them, not you!

Rule# 76

The "Like" Karma Rule

"I'm going to post some vacay pics soon. Time to give my friends lots of likes so the love loops back!"

—— The Logic ——

The more likes you spread, the more likes you'll be fed!

Ever feel like you're caught in a loop of likes on social media? The more likes you dish out, the more you get back. Every tap feels like a small generousity, and you deserve to be rewarded for your generousity, right?

Scrolling through your feed, tapping hearts like there's no tomorrow, it's all part of the game. You know those likes have a way of finding their way back to you. It's like the universe saying, "Hey, you've been spreading the love, so here's some love for you too." But it's not just about getting likes; it's about building connections in the digital world. Every heart you send out is like a heartbeat in the social media sphere, pulsing with the energy of virtual camaraderie. And when those likes come back to you, it's like a little digital high-five from your online tribe.

Of course, there's a fine art to mastering this. You have to find the sweet spot between being genuine and strategic, giving enough likes to show you care but not so many that you seem desperate for attention. It's a delicate balance, but when you get it right, the rewards are sweet.

So, the next time you're scrolling through your feed, remember: spread the love, and watch it come back to you in a digital dance of likes and notifications.   159

Rule# 77

The "Status" Intrigue Multiplier

"Updated my relationship status to 'It's complicated.' Watch out, drama queens, I'm taking the spotlight!"

—— The Logic ——

Add a little zest, make them guess!

"It's complicated" is for one reason only, an instant boost to your intrigue factor. It's like adding a pinch of spice to an otherwise bland dish. But why does it (and other mysterious status updates) work so well?

First off, let's talk about the allure of drama. We're living in the age of reality TV and viral scandals, where drama reigns supreme. By labeling your relationship as "It's complicated," you're tapping into that same thirst for excitement and unpredictability.

But it's also about independence. People love to put labels on everything, so declaring your relationship status as "It's complicated" is like sticking it to the man. You're refusing to be boxed in by society's expectations, and living life on your own terms.

And let's not forget about the practical benefits. Without potential love interests all over your social media, ambiguity is your friend. By keeping your relationship status vague, you're leaving room for interpretation, sparking curiosity in potential suitors. It's like leaving a trail of breadcrumbs for them to follow.

So, embrace the drama, assert your independence, and keep your options open. Sometimes it's good to keep them guessing. Why settle for simple when you can be gloriously, deliciously complicated? **161**

Rule # 78

You Can Have Many "Besties"

"Scarlet's been new at my work, like, five minutes, and bam! She's already in my top five besties."

—— The Logic ——

One BFF's fine, but why not have nine?

Ah, the unwritten rules of best-friendom, where the term "bestie" is as fluid as the latest TikTok trends. It's like trying to choose the best pizza toppings – ever-changing and open to interpretation. But hey, who says you can't have a whole squad of besties?

Picture this: you're at your favorite café, sipping on a pumpkin spice latte and pouring your heart out to one of your many besties. They're nodding along, offering sage advice, and reminding you why they're your ride-or-die. Sure, you might have a dozen other besties on speed dial, but this one is the "best".... for the moment.

And when it comes to loyalty, your besties are like a pack of fiercely protective wolves. In private, they'll call you out on your nonsense. But in front of anyone else – especially your significant other – they'll defend you to the ends of the earth.

From impromptu Netflix marathons to spontaneous road trips, everything is better with your besties by your side, turning the ordinary into the extraordinary. So here's to our besties – the ones who keep us laughing, loving, and living our best lives, one outrageous adventure at a time. Even though bestie means "best," with Girl Math, you can never have too many!

Rule# 79

The Group Date Upgrade

"Was worried Chad thought I was just a fling, but when he set up that night out with his friends, I knew I was in!"

—— The Logic ——

It's harder to bid adieu,
if his friends hang out with you!

The number of friends he invites on a group date is directly proportional to the seriousness of the relationship. Picture this: You've been casually dating someone for a while now. You've had your fair share of one-on-one dates, and things seem to be going pretty well. You haven't met the friends yet, but you've heard plenty about them. Then, out of the blue, your significant other drops the bombshell: you're going on a group date. At first, you think, "Okay, cool, a double date. That sounds fun." But then, as more details emerge, you realize it's not just a double date – it's a triple date. Three couples, all going out together. Suddenly, the intensity of the situation triples in an instant.

Your mind starts racing as you try to process what this means. It's a whole new level of relationship territory. After all, going on a group date means your significant other likes you enough to introduce you to their friends.

Fast forward a few years, and you're always in a group. Italy was all romantic and dreamy during year one, just you and your boo. But now? Now it's all about squad goals and group adventures. Cruises to the Caribbean with five other couples, beach bonfires with the whole gang, and luxury glamping trips. It's like the more, the merrier.

Rule# 80

The Social Approval Equation

"My new haircut got more likes than last time, so I'm sticking with it!"

—— The Logic ——

Comments and praise
will make anyone's ego' blaze!

More likes and comments on social media posts are more social validation, and just when you think you're above it and don't really care about all that, a post gets 2000 likes, and you can't help but love it!

Even if we don't want it be, every 'like' and 'share' is a badge of honor. You post a photo, throw in some witty hashtags, and cross your fingers, hoping for that sweet surge of validation. The struggle is real.

You spend hours crafting the perfect caption, agonizing over filters and edits, only to watch your post disappear into the abyss of the feed. It's like shouting into the void and hoping someone hears you.

And don't even get me started on the algorithm—it's like a fickle lover, constantly changing its mind and leaving you scrambling to keep up. One day, your post is on fire, racking up likes and shares like nobody's business. The next, it's crickets, as if the entire internet has collectively decided to ghost you.

But for every post that falls flat, there's a glimmer of hope—a comment from a friend, a share from a follower—that reminds you you're not alone in this digital wilderness. It's those moments of connection, those little sparks of human interaction, that make it all worthwhile.

167

Fun Fact:

Girls spend about 26% more time on social media apps than guys.

Guys are too busy doing useful things, like fantasy football.

Source: Statista.com (2021)

Bonus Chapter: Frugal Fancies and Household Hijinks

Rule # 81

The Overpacking Mandate

"5-day conference: 5 work fits + 5 evening vibes + 10 backups = suitcase packed for all-round success!"

—— The Logic ——

Better a big suitcase, than a fashion disgrace!

No matter how long your vacay, Girl Math decrees one must pack as though they're about to experience all four seasons, a surprise gala, and possibly an impromptu dip in a hot tub. I mean, what if you decide to go for a morning jog (for once)? Or what if you're suddenly invited to a fine dining night out? You have to think about these things when you're there, staring at your suitcase, realizing 15 pairs of undergarments for a 5-day trip is completely rational. It's basic math, really. Three for each day: one for the day, one in case you spill something, and one more… just because.

Then the outfits—A casual ensemble for exploring the city, a chic option for those Instagram-worthy café shots, and something glittery—because you never know when you'll need to be extra. Throw in a couple of 'maybe' dresses, 'I forgot I even owned this' tops, and 'I might finally wear this' shoes, and suddenly, you're playing Tetris with your suitcase.

And let's not forget the beauty arsenal. In goes the makeup bag that's suspiciously the size of a small country, filled with every conceivable shade of eyeshadow and lipstick, 'just in case' you need to match your look to your outfit, or your mood.

Sure the suitcase is half your body weight, but it's all worth it for the peace of mind, knowing that no matter what happens, you're prepared.

Rule# 82

DIY Is Cheaper Even When It's Not

"I definitely saved money making my own fall wreath, even if my bank account politely disagrees."

—— The Logic ——
If it was made with heart,
ignore the costly cart!

There's no better "spend more to flex" trap than a DIY project. You spot a project online and think, "Bet, why buy when I can DIY and flex my craft game?" Your shopping list starts chill but quickly hits boujee levels. Unicorn glitter, eco-vibes paper straws, and wood that costs more than your data plan—it adds up, and not in a cute way.

Home turns into a hot mess express, where you're the captain of the struggle bus, navigating through a sea of glitter and uncooperative fabric. Hours turn into "why did I start this" moments, but you push through. When it's all said and done, your creation is...a vibe. Definitely not store-bought, definitely not perfect, but it's got that DIY charm (read: it's a bit of a hot mess, but in a lovable way).

Here's the tea: checking your bank app reveals a total that's got you questioning your life choices. Could've been cheaper just buying the thing, but where's the fun in that?

So, you've got this unique piece that looks like it's seen some things, and your wallet's on a diet, but hey, you've earned some major DIY street cred. It's a wild ride, spending more for that "I made this" clout, but it's all about the story, the laughs, and that "I might do it again" attitude.

Rule# 83

The Half-Tank Hack

"Blew my budget on a shoe sale, so I'm rolling with half a tank to make my wallet smile again."

—— The Logic ——

Keep it in the bank, not in the tank!

Filling up just half the tank? Big brain move, right? It's like snagging a deal every time you hit the pump. Pay less now, feel rich—ignore that you're basically on a gas station tour by next week. Think of it as calorie counting but for your wallet. "I'll just fill up halfway," you say. It's genius, in a "I'll deal with it later" kind of way. Because who cares about more trips to the gas station? They're just more opportunities to save money again!

So yeah, filling up half the tank feels like a win. It's a masterclass in "out of sight, out of mind" finance. Paying less today makes us feel like budgeting pros, even if our bank accounts start side-eyeing us hard. It's all about that instant gratification, even if it means our gas light becomes a permanent fixture.

Plus, those extra stops? Perfect excuse for snack runs you didn't know you needed and mini-breaks in the day. While you're stopped and gas is flowing, you're only responsibility in life to entertain yourself with Instagram reels. Just don't get too lost in the feed and forget to stop the gas—keep that dollar figure cute.

Okay, so the actual savings might be up for debate, but trust me, the Girl Math checks out.

Rule # 84

Eternal Botanical Optimism

"Sure, I've dropped hundreds on now-dead plants, but this peace lily is totally my vibe!"

—— The Logic ——

Forget the wilted past, the next one will last!

There's a fierce belief that slaps back every time another exotic tropical plant catches our eye. "Okay, so I've hosted a few plant funerals, but this one? It's gonna slap, I'm pretty sure." Armed with TikTok tutorials and that one friend who actually remembers to water their plants, we're convinced: "This time it's on—This baby's gonna grow huge," ignoring the ghost of plant past.

Our optimism is our superpower. We turn our pads into tropical vibes central, where the air's stickier than a humid summer night. We're misting, chatting up our green pals, and reminding ourselves "Water, but don't drown, k?"

Each new plant is like a swipe right on Plant Tinder—a match made in hopeful heaven. We're the hype squad for photosynthesis, believing hard that this lil' dude will not just survive but straight-up thrive. "You and me, we got this," we whisper, tucking it into its new pot like it's the first day of school.

The cycle of buy, try, and sigh might be real, but so is our bounce-back game. With every new green addition, our squad of would-be green thumbs gets stronger, our Insta stories more hopeful. It's all about believing that this time, for real, we're gonna turn that apartment into a jungle oasis. And if not? There's always another plant waiting to prove us right.

Rule# 85

A New Car is Cheaper
Than Maintenance

"A headlight went out and I'm like, 'Well, that's practically half the monthly cost of a new BMW, right?'"

—— The Logic ——

A scratch, a dent, time for that new car scent!

The sight of a single dashboard warning light can send us spiraling into, "Time for a New Car!" It's as if every minor hiccup with our trusty steeds is a divine signal from the car gods whispering, "Why fix it when you can upgrade it?"

You're jamming to your playlist, and suddenly one speaker starts sounding like it's been possessed by a 90s dial-up modem. The average dude might think, "Oh, a quick fix!" But, oh no, not us. Our minds race to, "This sound system's hiccup clearly means the car's entire electronic system is iffy!" Because the leap from a crackly speaker to a full automotive overhaul is just a small skip in Girl Math land. Our inner drama queen sees every problem as a reason to browse the latest car models. "Check Engine? More like check out the new car catalogs."

God forbid your friend gets a new car that can practically drive itself. Suddenly, every minor feature lacking on your own car is amplified. Automated drink warmers, are you kidding? Why live in the past when the present is offering luxury spaceships?

In the end, it's a testament to our unwavering belief in fresh starts (and perhaps our fear of car maintenance). But isn't life too short not to entertain the idea of new possibilities on four wheels, even if our "logic" might have others chuckling?

Rule# 86

TV vs Movie:
The Commitment Contrast

"A 2 hr movie? That's like a whole commitment. Now excuse me while I start season 1 of 5."

—— The Logic ——

Bite—sized hours are easy to devour!

It's a classic early Sunday evening. The weekend's whirlwind of fun, complete with Saturday's hangover and Sunday's chore marathon, is winding down. With the 'Sunday Scaries' creeping up, all you crave is a slice of peace before the workweek. So, there you are, curled up in your coziest spot, armed with Chinese takeout—calories magically canceled out by your choice of flavored seltzer water.

He suggests a movie. "How about this one?" he says, pointing to a 2 hours and 45 minute saga. "Are you out of your mind?" you counter. There's no way you're signing up for a three-hour commitment when Monday is breathing down your neck. Instead, you steer him toward that new true crime series on Netflix you've both been eyeing. "It's perfect," you assure him, "just a few episodes."

Six hours later, you're both still glued to the screen, the plot thickens, and cliffhangers have you in a vice grip. It's way past your usual bedtime. "Just one more," you both agree, as the rules of time and responsibility seem to dissolve.

The irony isn't lost on you: earlier, a single movie felt like a marathon, but now you've completed an ultra-marathon. You even finish it with the satisfaction of time well spent!

Rule # 87

Cosmetics Are Costless

"Gave up online courses for a chem peel because it'll pay dividends before a degree ever will!"

—— The Logic ——

If it makes you shine, the price is fine!

Cosmetic upgrades and skincare splurges are like opening a savings account where the interest rate is measured in confidence. Dropping a small fortune on serums and fillers is like buying stock in your own glow-up. So when you eye that $300 moisturizer, don't just rationalize it as "less than a dollar a day"—frame it as your personal fountain of youth, on a payment plan. Why save money when you can save something priceless—your skin?

Cosmetic procedures are not expenses; they're capital improvements. We're funding our future selves, ensuring our faces and bodies appreciate in value like a rare vintage wine. "Why yes, I'll take the anti-aging package. Can I set up a direct deposit from my paycheck right to my face?"

Every glance in the mirror is a review of our investment assets. Fine lines? Just a market fluctuation. A new laugh line? Think of it as the market correcting itself. And when our skin glows? That's the bull market we've been investing in.

So, next time someone questions your high-dollar skincare routines, just remember: you're being financially savvy. After all, if beauty is power, consider us the Warren Buffetts of the beauty world, building our empire one collagen peptide at a time.

Rule # 88

Bailing Equals Making Money

"Ditched the concert and sold my ticket on StubHub. Even if it was half what I paid, I profited!"

—— The Logic ——

Canceled plans are cash in your hands!

Canceling plans might be a last-minute decision, but it's also a great way to "make" money! You've been eyeing that fancy new restaurant downtown, and you're all set to go, outfit picked out, reservations made. But then, a moment of brilliance strikes. What if you just... didn't?

Suddenly, it's not just an evening freed up; it's a windfall. You've just made a killing by not spending a dime. Who knew that financial success could be as simple as saying, "Actually, let's just stay in"? It's like finding free money that is probably equivalent to a week's worth of groceries. Your bank account swells with pride.

And let's not forget the added bonuses. The money you didn't spend on that Uber ride? The tip you didn't leave because the waiter is pretty cute? That's dividends paying out in real-time. The friends you ditched? They're just co-investors in this scheme. The true genius lies in the art of the follow-up. A simple "Let's catch up soon, my treat!" keeps the social ledger balanced. It's a promissory note, and if executed with grace, it turns potential social bankruptcy into an investment in future gatherings.

So, the next time you find yourself backing out of dinner plans, remember: you're not being flaky; you're being financially savvy!

Fun Fact:

On average, girls spend about 5 ½ hours more per week than their partners on housework.

Or as boys call it, "Fair."

Source: BLS.gov (2022)

Girl Math Reflections

Congratulations! You've made it to the end of this whimsical journey through the world of illogical logic and rational irrationality.

Throughout this book, we've laughed, we've nodded knowingly, and perhaps we've even cringed at some of the absurdities of Girl Math. But beyond the humor, there's a valuable lesson to be learned.

Girl Math is a reminder that sometimes, our minds play tricks on us, leading us to make decisions that defy logic. But amidst the chaos, there's beauty in our ability to find humor in our own irrationality, to embrace our quirks, and to celebrate the unique way we each navigate the world.

So, dear reader, as you close this book and return to your own adventures, I invite you to carry the spirit of Girl Math with you. Reflect on your own experiences with Girl Math, share your favorite rules with friends, and let's continue to find joy in the absurdities of life together.

Don't forget to tag your favorite rules with #GirlMathBook and spread the laughter far and wide!

If this book brought joy, laughter, or a smile to you,

Leave a Rating or a Review!

Scan Here